The **Mini Rough Guide** to

COPENHAGEN

I0806708

ROUGH GUIDES

How to download your Free eBook

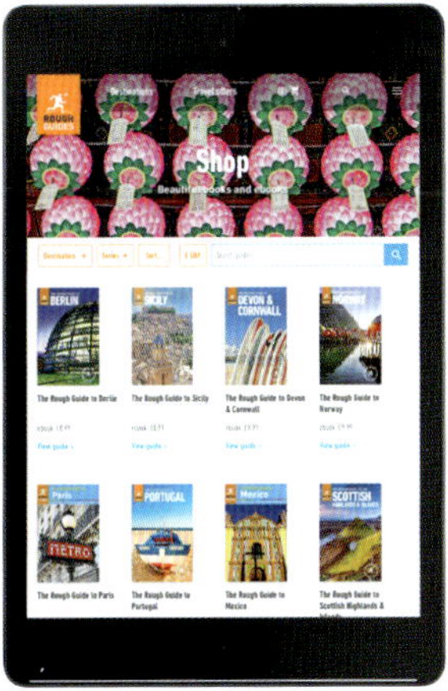

1. Visit **www.roughguides.com/free-ebook** or scan the **QR code** opposite

2. Enter the code **copenhagen993**

3. Follow the simple step-by-step instructions

For troubleshooting contact: mail@roughguides.com

Contents

Introduction

Copenhagen (København), the capital of Denmark, is a charming seaside city with captivating architecture, history, culture, quirks and extraordinary cuisine. From some of the best restaurants in the world to budget street-eats. Water is everywhere – the city is located on the eastern side of Zealand, the largest of Denmark's 400-plus islands, with only a narrow body of salt-sea, the Øresund (Strait), separating it from Sweden. Around 2 million of the country's population of 6 million call Copenhagen (and its surrounding metropolitan area) home. This compact little city heads a compact nation: Denmark itself is the smallest yet most densely populated nation in northern Europe, with over six times as many people per square kilometre as neighbouring Sweden.

WHAT'S NEW

A surge of exciting launches and reopenings has swept the city in recent years, among these revamped editions of the Danish Jewish Museum, Home of Carlsberg, Museum of Danish Resistance and ENIGMA (the Museum of Communication), having in its latest iteration branched far beyond its roots as a tribute to the postal service. Since 2023, when Copenhagen was named UNESCO's World Capital of Architecture, the Danish Architecture Centre has housed the excellent 'So Danish!' gallery, showcasing the history of this veritable Danish passion. Another highlight not to miss is the central Museum of Copenhagen, tapped by one newspaper of record in 2024 as perhaps 'the city's best museum' for its powerful, intimate telling of the city's story. Beyond its growing list of sights, Copenhagen continues to expand its menu of world-class restaurants, performance venues and activities, both indoors and outdoors: from gallery hopping to urban swimming to skiing – yes, skiing! – on the roof of a cutting-edge plant (see page 99), one reflection among many of the city's ambition to reach carbon neutrality by 2025.

Canalside nightlife along Nyhavn

Denmark is the only Scandinavian country physically connected to the European mainland – the Jutland peninsula is joined to northern Germany – and it forms both a literal and metaphorical bridge between Scandinavia and the rest of the continent. Denmark shares many of the characteristics of its Nordic neighbours: liberal welfare benefits coupled with a

NOTES

Denmark has the oldest royal dynasty in Europe, harkening back to the rule of Harald Bluetooth, the Viking chieftain who unified Denmark over a millennium ago. For more than half a century from 1972, the dynasty's first reigning queen was Queen Margrethe II, who abdicated the throne to her son, King Frederik X since January 2024.

Café culture in Copenhagen

high standard of living, and a style of government that aims at consensus. Yet the country is also more 'European' than the rest of Scandinavia, and its appeal is universal.

Cosmopolitan Charm

Long before the phrase was immortalised in song by Danny Kaye, Copenhagen was known to be 'wonderful, wonderful' – a clean, green city full of gaiety, culture and charm, with a tradition of tolerance and humour.

In 1167, Bishop Absalon built a coastal castle at Havn, a strategic location at the mouth of the Baltic. Over the centuries, a city grew up around it, and Copenhagen became the seat of royalty and the cultural and political centre that it is today. The green copper towers of churches, castles and cathedrals are scattered across the skyline – wander through cobbled streets and courtyards to discover the Christiansborg complex, Rosenborg Slot and the Amalienborg palaces, and a multitude of museums explaining their significance. Convivial Danes have made an art of the cosy coffee shop, and the city boasts some of the world's finest restaurants. Copenhagen is also renowned as one of northern Europe's jazz capitals – lively music and summer sunshine accompany shoppers as they stroll along Strøget, the longest pedestrianised street in the world. Its varied array of stores offer everything from handmade chocolates to cutting-edge clothing to Danish-designed homeware and furniture.

The People

Embodying a sense of 'cosiness' and the generally sociable character of Danes, the Danish word *hygge* entered the global lexicon during the 2010s, conveying a combination of warmth, wellbeing and intimacy. Consistently counted among the world's happiest peoples, Danes incorporate *hygge* into their lives as much as

WHEN TO GO

Easily Copenhagen's best season is summer, when both locals and visitors make the most of the long days and ideal weather to stay out late nursing drinks through the wee hours. It's also the period that enjoys the bulk of the city's cultural events, among them the ten-day-long Copenhagen Jazz Festival, bringing live music, dance and art to the streets. Autumn and spring are similarly alluring – especially for cycling – since the afternoons remain warm but the majority of tourists have departed. Still, don't write off winter, a perfectly charming time for drinking *gløgg* (Scandinavian mulled wine) in cosy bars and enjoying the beloved Danish tradition of *hygge* (cosiness). The festive markets of Tivoli and Nyhavn and the Christmas lights make the city an excellent destination for a festive break.

SUSTAINABLE TRAVEL

Repeatedly ranking among the world's happiest, most liveable cities, Copenhagen made waves with its 2024 trial run of an innovative approach to sustainable tourism, humorously dubbed 'Copenpay'. Through the tourism bureau's scheme, the city pledged to reward eco-conscious behaviour with free food, drinks and complimentary tickets at city attractions. But it's easy enough, with or without such incentives, to responsibly enjoy this city. In terms of transport, there's a highly walkable core and an excellent network of bike lanes, buses and trains; renting a car is just a hassle. (When opting to cycle, however, be careful to stick to the bike lanes and use the proper signals.) When it comes to food, Copenhagen's best restaurants – like Geranium – are pioneers in sustainable, locally-sourced dining. Environmental consciousness, however, has spread well beyond the elite fine dining class in this city, with plant-based options easily found almost anywhere in town. Immersive, sustainable experiences are also plentiful: meet real-life Danes pitching in at an urban farm like Øens Have (oenshave.dk), or clean up rubbish while enjoying a self-steered tour of the city's canals (greenkayak.org).

possible. A sense of *hygge* can be felt in every part of Copenhagen, but is more obvious, especially on public holidays and warm sunny days, in the city's many green spaces such as Rosenborg Have, Ørstedsparken, Tivoli Gardens and popular meeting places like Rådhuspladsen and Nyhavn. As much as beers in the park during summer with friends or canal-side lounging, *hygge* can mean mugs of hot chocolate, thick scarves, cosey cafés or candles reflected in windows, effectively quashing the gloom of the year's longest nights.

Out and About

Within a very short distance of Copenhagen, and easily accessible on day trips, are three several major places of interest:

Roskilde, with its superb cathedral and unmissable Viking Ship Museum; Hillerød's beautiful Frederiksborg Castle; and Helsingør's Kronborg Castle, known to Shakespeare fans as Hamlet's home, Elsinore. Also worth a trip are Dragør, a picturesque fishing village near the airport; and the Louisiana Museum of Modern Art at Humlebæk, in a sublime setting on the picturesque coast just north of Copenhagen.

Sweden is just 4km (2.5 miles) away from Denmark at the narrowest point of the Øresund. The Swedish town of Helsingborg is a half-hour sail from Helsingør on one of the numerous ferries that ply the Sound. Malmø can be reached by road or rail over the Øresund Bridge in just 35 minutes.

Cycling is a popular way to get around in Copenhagen

1

2

3

10 Things not to miss

4

5

6

1 **CHRISTIANSBORG**
See the equestrian statue of Christian IX at the seat of the Danish Parliament. See page 46.

2 **AMALIENBORG SLOT**
On duty at the home of the royal family. See page 63.

3 **TORVEHALLERNE**
Build up an appetite at this food market with food stalls and local producers. See page 112.

4 **KIRKE**
Marvel at its spiralling staircase and copper-clad tower. See page 71.

5 **NYHAVN**
Copenhagen's colourful harbour, lined with bars and restaurants. See page 61.

6 **ROSENBORG SLOT**
The 17th-century palace houses the crown jewels. See page 57.

7 **NATIONALMUSEET**
Home of the famous Trundholm Sun Chariot. See page 52.

8 **ROSKILDE**
Visit Denmark's Viking heritage at this neat little town nearby. See page 86.

9 **NY CARLSBERG GLYPTOTEK**
In a distinctive building lies one of the world's foremost collections of classical art. See page 54.

10 **TIVOLI GARDENS**
The night-time illuminations are among its many attractions. See page 33.

A perfect day in Copenhagen

9AM

Breakfast. To start off the day, do as the Danes do and pick up a *bolle med ost* (simple sourdough roll with butter and cheese) or, if it's something a little sweeter you're after, a *spandauer* (custard-filled Danish pastry).

10AM

Hit the shops. Stroll along pedestrianised Strøget, peeking into shop windows and making forays into the surrounding cobbled streets. Pop into Royal Copenhagen to admire Danish-designed home furnishings, silverware and porcelain, earmarking your favourites to purchase later.

11AM

Coffee. Cross Kongens Nytorv and head for the pretty painted wharf side at Nyhavn, one of the city's best people-watching places. Sit outside with a mid-morning coffee and watch the world go by.

11.30AM

Little Mermaid. Tick her off your list by hopping aboard one of the 60-minute canal-boat tours, which depart from Nyhavn and sail all the way along the harbour.

12.30PM

Lunchtime. Time to eat again! Wander along the harbour-side towards Frederiksholms canal, taking time to appreciate the Black Diamond and the buildings of Slotsholmen, before lunching on *smørrebrød* in the highly atmospheric Kanal Caféen (reservations are a must).

2PM

Culture fix. Spend a few hours exploring Danish history and culture, according to your interests. You're now very close to the fabulous Ny Carlsberg Glyptotek, the Museum of Copenhagen, Christiansborg and the National Museum.

7PM

Dinner. Cross the harbour onto Christianshavn for a pre-dinner evening stroll around the always-interesting Christiania. You can eat at Spiseloppen, a delightfully cosy restaurant inside the Free Town; or treat yourself at the nearby, double Michelin-starred Kadeau (again, book ahead!).

8PM

Opera. The stunning Opera House is on this side of the harbour – get your fix of Puccini or Bizet in a building so ultra-modern you'll hardly know whether to look at the action on stage or the architecture.

11PM

On the town. At 11pm, Copenhagen's youth are just beginning to head out to the city's bars and clubs. The Vesterbro district is good for nightlife – its lively Kødbyen area is the coolest place to laugh, drink and dance until the early hours.

Royal Copenhagen

10AM

Christiansborg Palace. Start your day on the site of Absalons Borg, Copenhagen's ground zero: Christiansborg Palace. Head through the complex's imposing gateway, directly beneath its central tower. Glimpse the royal stables and, if open, don't miss the sumptuous Royal Reception Rooms, occasionally graced by the King and Prime Minister to greet foreign dignitaries.

11.15AM

The Royal Residence. Using the Line 3 metro (from the adjacent Gammelstrand station to Marmor station), reach the home of the Danish royal family. Get a further glimpse into kingly life at the Amalienborg Palace Museum, wrapping up your visit before noon, when the daily changing of the guard takes place.

12.30PM

The Marble Church. Make a beeline for the grandiose dome of the neo-Baroque Marmorkirken (the Marble Church), named for its founder Frederik V.

1PM

Royal Navy Quarters. Cross Store Kongensgade to admire the yellow-painted, 17th-century homes of Nyboder. Though apparently purpose-built for Instagrammers, it was commissioned by King Christian IV as housing for the Royal Navy. Hit Fredericiagade en route to your next stop for lunch or to stock up on picnic supplies.

2PM

Kongens Have & Rosenborg Castle. Traverse the gorgeous grounds of Kongens Have ('The King's Garden'), perhaps claiming a bench or your own patch of grass for a picnic. A superlative people-watching spot, it centres around the beautiful Rosenborg Castle, another monument with roots tracing back to the illustrious Christian IV. Today, it's home to a museum displaying the eye-popping royal treasury.

4PM

Rundetaarn. A short hop to the south of Kongens Have you'll reach the forbidding Round Tower, where you can climb its spiral ramp to the roof for wonderful views of the city in all directions.

4.30PM

Church of Our Lady. After a stroll down busy Strøget, step into the calm of Vor Frue Kirke (Church of Our Lady), dominated by the sculptural works of Bertel Thorvaldsen. As the city's main cathedral, it's a favourite for royal weddings.

5.30PM

Street food. Head north along Nørregade to be spoiled for choice at the city's best street food market. Opened in 2011, Torvehallerne is admittedly not the work of Christian IV, but the cosmopolitan monarch would no doubt approve of the dizzying selection of cuisines on offer.

Riding the Circle Line

8.30AM

Østerport. Just a few stops north of the city's central station, København H, alight from the metro at Østerport station. Grab a pastry or snack at the nextdoor supermarket bakery before circling Copenhagen's sprawling Citadel, passing the charming St. Alban's Church en route, as well as the striking Gefion Fountain and the iconic Little Mermaid statue.

10AM

Trianglen. Plan for your arrival to coincide with the opening time of one of Copenhagen's most thought-provoking museums: ENIGMA, dedicated to the history of communication, opened here at the edge of the city's largest park in 2023.

11.30AM

Skjolds Plads. Take the metro three stops, then right outside Skjolds Plads station hop on the 6A bus (departs every 5min) to Grundtvigs Kirke, an architectural marvel both inside and out. Just opposite is the Bispebjerg Cemetery, which explodes with cherry blossoms in April and May.

1.30PM

Nørrebros Runddel. Return on the 6A to Skjolds Plads (or take the 4A bus to Nørrebro station; departs every 7 minutes), continuing your metro journey to Nørrebros Runddel, at the heart of youthful Nørrebro. Take your pick among the superlative restaurants packing Nørrebrogade just opposite the station, then wander the eminent Assistens Kirkegård, easily the city's most famous cemetery, perhaps even paying respects at the graves of Søren Kierkegaard, Niels Bohr and Hans Christian Andersen.

3.30PM

Frederiksberg. It's a short walk south from Frederiksberg station to the rambling, green retreat of Frederiksberg Have, where you can search for its resident herons on the path to its former royal palace, Frederiksberg Slot. If it's open, the city's old cisterns just past the park – now an evocative art space – are also worth a peek. Continue south on foot to the Home of Carlsberg, where a cold beer – well-earned – is included in the brewery's tour covering the history and production process.

5.30PM

København H. Rejoin Cityringen for a final leg from Enghave Plads station to complete the circle at København H, at the edge of the ultra-hip Meatpacking District: Kødbyen. Rightfully known for its nightlife, it's also an excellent place to find yourself at dinnertime. Choose from sourdough pizzas at Mother or delicious street tacos at Hija de Sanchez, or keep things old-school Danish by ordering *flæskesteg* (pork roast) at the down-to-earth Chicky Grill Bar.

History

Well before the Vikings organised themselves into an extraordinary nation of seafarers, Denmark was inhabited by hunting peoples. Prehistoric relics of all kinds – some dating back to 50,000 BC – are displayed in Copenhagen's museums. The oldest surviving costumes in Europe have been found in this area, as have various musical instruments, including more than 30 examples of the Danish lur, which emits hoarse notes that seem strangely out of keeping with the long, graceful S-shaped stem characteristic of the instrument.

Viking Age

The first written records of the Vikings appear around AD 800, at which time Viking raids on neighbouring European countries were becoming notorious. These fearless warriors reached Newfoundland, rounded the North Cape and made sallies to Britain, Holland, France, Spain and the Mediterranean, endeding up as far afield as Russia, North Africa and the Middle East. Examples of their boats are on display at the Roskilde Viking Ship Museum (see page 88).

Danish raids upon England gathered in strength during the late 10th century and the first years of the 11th century, culminating in an attempt at conquest. Canute (Knud) the Great, after meeting considerable resistance, finally became King of England in 1016. The union was to last until 1042.

Christianity had been introduced into Denmark in 826 by a Benedictine monk, and received the royal seal of approval in 961 when King Harald (Bluetooth)

NOTES

For a visual account of the city's colourful past and its better-known characters, call into Københavns Museum (The Museum of Copenhagen; Stormgade 18; www.cphmuseum.kk.dk).

converted. He had his legacy engraved on a large runic stone at Jelling in East Jutland, which records that Harald had 'won for himself all Denmark and Norway and made the Danes Christians'.

The equestrian statue of Bishop Absalon on Højbro Plads

Medieval Times

In 1157, Valdemar I (the Great) came to the throne. He leaned heavily on the influence of Bishop Absalon of Roskilde, and this proved a partnership of critical importance to Copenhagen, then just a little fishing village called Havn. With its fine harbour on the Strait (Øresund in Danish) between Denmark and Sweden, the village was strategically placed at the entrance to the Baltic Sea, then emerging as a major trade hub.

War hero as well as statesman, Bishop Absalon fortified Havn by constructing a castle on its small harbour island of Slotsholmen in 1167, now acknowledged as the founding date of the modern city. The name Havn became Køpmannæhafn ('merchants' harbour') in 1170, and eventually København. Today, Slotsholmen hosts the impressive Christiansborg parliament buildings, but you can see some intriguing remnants of Absalon's castle in their cellars (see page 49).

By the 13th century, the ascendant Danish nobility managed to curb the powers of the monarchy, forcing King Erik V to sign a

Great Charter in 1282. Under this arrangement, often referred to as Denmark's very first constitution, the King would rule together with the nobles in the Council of the Danish Realm.

Nevertheless, Valdemar IV Atterdag (*c.*1320–75), probably the greatest of medieval Danish kings, led the country back onto a path of conquests and into new conflict with its Nordic neighbours, setting a pattern that was to last, intermittently, for centuries. Denmark's hand was greatly strengthened when Valdemar's daughter Margrete married Håkon VI, King of Norway and Sweden. After his death, Margrete succeeded through the Treaty of Kalmar in 1397 in unifying the three Nordic powers under her great-nephew Erik VII of Pomerania. Indomitable Margrete ruled in his name, but was struck down by the plague at the peak of her power in 1412.

During the later, true reign of Erik VII (1412–39), Copenhagen was enlarged. The city became the official Danish capital under Christopher III of Bavaria in the 1440s, and when a university was founded by Christian I in 1479, it also became the country's cultural centre, its population by then having increased to about 10,000 inhabitants. To the north at Helsingør (the Elsinore of Shakespeare's *Hamlet*), a castle was built to enforce the payment of tolls on the Øresund, control of which was strategically vital to Denmark. Dues were exacted from each ship passing through the 4km (2.5-mile) wide channel between Helsingør on Zealand and Helsingborg in Sweden.

BISHOP ABSALON

Absalon (1128–1201), Bishop of Roskilde, Archbishop of Lund and founder of Copenhagen, was also a statesman, a crusader against the terrorising Wends, and a literary patron. His foster brother, Valdemar I, granted him the fishing village of Havn where Absalon built a stronghold on the site now occupied by Christiansborg (see page 46). The bishop commissioned his secretary, Saxo Grammaticus, to produce *Gesta Danorum*, an invaluable history of Denmark.

While Denmark enjoyed a very strong position, the next 200 years proved a turbulent period. It was marked by civil war, the advent of Lutheranism, and Sweden's undying enmity following the infamous 1520 'Stockholm Bloodbath', when Danish King Christian II slaughtered 82 Swedish elite at a banquet. This mass execution provoked the Swedish War of Liberation: the Kalmar Union collapsed. Sweden proclaimed its independence, though Denmark and Norway remained united.

The Danish Crown Jewels on display in Rosenborg Castle

The Reformation

In the 16th century, a latent, deep-seated discontent regarding abuses within the Catholic Church began to spill out into the open. In Denmark, Catholic bishops had long funded political and military endeavors. But in 1536, Christian III (1534–59) declared himself supreme authority of a state church based on Lutheranism, a Protestant branch which had already made deep inroads since arriving from Germany. The bishops were imprisoned until they 'consented'.

Meanwhile, the wars with Sweden lurched disastrously on. By the latter half of the 17th century Denmark had been forced to relinquish her remaining Swedish possessions, including the east bank of the Øresund. This crucial waterway was now jointly controlled by the two Scandinavian powers, as remains the case today.

As Denmark licked its wounds, the city of Copenhagen enjoyed two consolations. Firstly, the 60-year reign of larger-than-life Christian IV (1588–1648) saw a wave of new culture and fine architecture sweep the city. The 'Great Builder' doubled the size of Copenhagen, constructing many of its beautiful Renaissance buildings, among them the Round Tower, Børsen (the Stock Exchange) and Rosenborg Castle. Then, in 1660, Copenhagen was declared a free city as an acknowledgement of its bravery during a two-year blockade by Sweden, meaning that all its residents were accorded the same privileges as the nobles.

Absolute Power

As with the ongoing conflict with Sweden, involvement in the Thirty Years' War was hugely damaging for Denmark. By the time of the death of King Christian IV, the country was bankrupt and greatly reduced, a situation inevitably sparking widespread discontent throughout the country. In response, King Frederik III proclaimed himself absolute monarch in 1660, thereby depriving the nobles of the Council of the Danish Realm of the powers they had enjoyed since 1282. Frederik's absolute rule coincided with a period of national unity, with a tightly controlled, well-organised central bureaucracy.

The early absolutist kings continued to wage costly wars, mainly against Sweden. Copenhagen suffered a terrible plague in 1711–12 which killed 22,000 people – nearly a third of its inhabitants – as well as two devastating fires in 1728 and 1795.

The 18th century saw major social change. Serfdom was abolished in 1788 (note the Freedom Pillar in Vesterbrogade, opposite the Central Station) and peasants threw off the yoke of the medieval landlord and began to work for themselves. This emancipation gave the Danish countryside its present character of a landscape dotted with farms, and was of enormous influence in the shaping of modern Denmark.

Napoleon and the 19th Century

Denmark found itself reluctantly involved in the revolutionary wars of late-18th-century Europe. It attracted the wrath of the British by participating in the League of Armed Neutrality, an alliance with Russia, Sweden and Prussia aimed at preventing Great Britain from searching neutral vessels at sea. In 1801, a fleet under admirals Nelson and Parker sailed into the bay of Copenhagen. During the ensuing battle, Nelson, so legend has it, raised a telescope to his blind eye so that he could deny having seen the signal to break off the engagement.

In 1807, fearing a takeover of the Dano-Norwegian fleet by Napoleon, Britain demanded its surrender. When the Danes refused, Copenhagen was blockaded and bombarded for three days, leaving the Danes little choice but to surrender what was left of its fleet to the British Navy, only to be forced immediately afterwards into an alliance with Napoleon, who was by then marching fast into Jutland. When Napoleon was finally brought to his knees, Denmark emerged completely isolated on account of this alliance. To pay off its war debts, Norway was handed to Sweden in 1814. Denmark's overseas territories were now limited to Greenland, Iceland, the Faroes and the

The Battle of Copenhagen, April 1801

N.F.S. Grundtvig, priest, writer and pioneering educationalist

Virgin Islands. Fifty years later Denmark was further reduced by the loss of the duchies of Schleswig and Holstein – a third of its home territory and two-fifths of its population – to Bismarck's Prussia. Following a spate of civil turmoil in Denmark provoked by the 1848 revolution in France, Frederik VII was forced to relinquish absolute rule and hand over the reins of power to the National Liberal Party.

A liberal constitution was drawn up with wide suffrage, and the Danish 'Golden Age' was all set to begin. In the city, Hans Christian Andersen (1805–75), the writer from Odense, strolled the streets, reading his fairy tales to fans. Factories and housing blocks for workers sprang up, so that by the late 19th century Copenhagen was a thriving industrial centre. A growing sense of civic pride and national identity swept both city and countryside, fed by the reforms of the theologian and politician N.F.S. Gruntvig (1783–1872), having introduced a system of popular adult high schools to improve the peasant's lot.

The 20th Century

In 1901 an important landmark was reached in Danish constitutional history when a government based only on a majority in the lower chamber of parliament (Folketing) was appointed. The march of the common people brought them not only into the cities and urban areas, but also right into the political struggle. In 1915, the Liberal Democrats, Social Democrats and Radical Liberals jointly forced the abolition of electoral privileges in the upper chamber and initiated a system of proportional representation for both chambers. At the same time, the vote was at last given to women and servants.

After the World War I, in which Denmark retained its neutrality, north Schleswig voted itself back into the country, establishing the shape of today's border. Industrial unrest and economic depression in the interwar years failed to halt Danish progress. In the design of consumer goods (furniture, cutlery, glass, pewter, silver and textiles) Denmark set new standards, combining utility with beauty. Indeed, 'Danish design' became synonymous with good, functional, yet aesthetically pleasing articles.

On 9 April 1940, despite Scandinavian declarations of neutrality at the outset of World War II, Denmark was invaded by Germany, putting up only token resistance. However, the anti-Nazi sentiments of the vast majority of Danes were expressed by cold-shoulder treatment, and eventually acted upon through outright resistance. The Danes managed by various means to smuggle 7,000 of Denmark's 7,500 Jews out of the country and into neighbouring Sweden. The wartime king Christian X elected to remain in Denmark during the Nazi occupation, becoming a symbol of independence and resistance.

The end of the war in 1945 ushered in a new era of massive Danish reconstruction, resulting in the prosperous society seen today – one of the world's most successful attempts at a modern welfare state.

Politically, Denmark abandoned neutrality when it became a member of NATO in 1949. Economically, it was a founding member of the European Free Trade Association (EFTA), and joined the European Economic Community (subsequently the European Union) with the UK and Ireland in 1972.

Strolling in Kongens Have (the King's Garden)

Modern Denmark

Regularly appearing at the top of lists of the happiest countries on earth, Denmark is home to around 6 million people and enjoys an extremely high standard of living. But no place is perfect. Immigration over the years has consistently challenged Danish notions of tolerance. In 2001, right-wing parties on a platform of anti-immigration and law and order formed a coalition government that endured until 2011. By 2015, the issue had returned to the forefront with the European migrant crisis, occurring amidst a surge in Islamist violence across the continent, leading to more restrictive immigration policies, among them increased border controls. In the wake of the 2019 elections, Social Democrat Mette Frederiksen emerged victorious, her popularity based on not only a tough approach to immigration, but plans to increase public spending and cut greenhouse gas emissions by 70 percent by 2030. During the pandemic, Denmark's relatively hard lockdowns were ended earlier than elsewhere, but Frederiksen drew harsh critique (and a formal investigation) for her order to cull Denmark's 17 million minks over COVID fears. Only the second female to serve as the Danish Prime Minister, Frederiksen became the first to win a second term in 2022, and the only one yet to serve under the reign of King Frederik X, crowned on 14 January 2024.

Chronology

1167 Absalon fortifies the fishing and trading settlement of Havn.
1254 The village of Køpmannæhafn receives a municipal charter.
1376 Absalon's castle is replaced by København Slot.
1397–1534 Denmark sets up the Kalmar Union with Norway and Sweden.
1417 Erik VII makes Copenhagen his capital.
1479 The university is founded by Christian I.
1588–1648 Christian IV enlarges the town and harbour, commissioning grand Renaissance-style buildings.
1660 Copenhagen is declared a free city.
1711–12 Plague kills nearly one third of Copenhagen's inhabitants.
Early 1800s The British fleet under Nelson bombards the city for three days.
Late 1800s Denmark's 'Golden Age' of arts and science.
1914–18 Denmark remains neutral during World War I.
1918 Christiansborg Palace becomes the seat of the Danish parliament.
1924 Social Democrats win power; a welfare state is established.
1940–5 Denmark is occupied by German forces.
1973 Denmark joins the European Economic Community (EEC), which becomes the European Union in 1993.
2000 The Øresund Bridge is opened. By referendum, Denmark opts to retain the krone rather than adopting the euro.
2005–6 'Muhammad drawings' in the *Jyllands-Posten* newspaper spur a major diplomatic crisis and an ongoing debate on free speech.
2015 An Islamist gunman kills two people in separate attacks at a free speech event in a café and at a synagogue in Copenhagen.
2016 Parliament backs a controversial bill to confiscate asylum seekers' cash and valuables to cover housing and food costs.
2018 Denmark bans wearing face veils in public.
2024 On 14 January, Queen Margrethe abdicates the throne to her son, King Frederik X, after exactly 52 years as monarch.

The Danish Royal Library

Places

You will have no problem finding your way around this delightfully compact city. Most of the important sights and museums are contained within the central section and bounded by the former medieval ramparts, so exploring Copenhagen on foot is a real pleasure. The network of canals also offers many opportunities for waterside walks and gentle excursions afloat. And if you want a change of pace from sightseeing or shopping, the abundance of leafy parks and attractive gardens provides a very welcome and pleasant retreat.

Around Rådhuspladsen and Vesterbro

Highlights

- **City Hall**, see page 32
- **Lurs and Legends**, see page 33
- **Tivoli Gardens**, see page 33
- **Vesterbro**, see page 36

Every city has a social gathering point, but Copenhagen has more than one. Without a doubt, the centrally located **Rådhuspladsen** (City Hall Square) is the most popular and, consequently, most of the suggested planned walks start from here. It is also the stopping point for the main bus routes and is near Central Station, where trains depart for the suburbs and beyond.

It is in this large open square, with its buskers

NOTES

Museum opening times and charges are subject to change. It is advisable to check the listings at www.visitcopenhagen.com or www.copenhagen.com. The Copenhagen Card (see page 137) offers free or discounted entry.

and ubiquitous hot-dog stands *(pølsevogn)*, that you can take the opportunity to observe Danish life.

City Hall

The dominant building in Rådhuspladsen is the red-brick **Rådhus** ❶ (City Hall; www.kk.dk; free), with its 105m (345ft) tower. Built between 1892 and 1905, it is reached via broad steps which play host to impromptu concerts. Its main doorway is crowned by a statue of Bishop Absalon, the founder of the city, in copper and 22-carat gilt. On the roof above you'll see six bronze figures of night watchmen dating from various periods of the city's history. Each section of the Rådhus bears a different style and imprint, but

Rådhuspladsen, focal point of city life

they come together architecturally very much like a patchwork quilt. The main hall and banqueting room are impressive with their statuary and coats-of-arms – especially the view of the 44m (145ft) long hall from the first-floor colonnade (guided tours in English Mon–Fri 1pm, Sat 10am; www.kk.dk).

If you are feeling energetic, there are also guided tours of **City Hall Tower** and its 300 steps (check website for available times). On a clear day you can see north along the coast and across the Øresund to Sweden. In the foyer of City Hall a sign points to **Jens Olsen's World Clock** (free). This intriguing astronomical clock, said to have more than 14,000 parts, shows time around the world, the positions of the planets and the Gregorian calendar.

Lurs and Legends

To your right as you leave the City Hall, on Vester Voldgade, is the unique **Lur Players** statue. Legend has it that the two men on top will sound a note on their instruments if a virgin passes by – they've been standing on the column since 1914 but have led a life of silence. On the opposite corner of the square is the dramatic copper **Bull-and-Dragon Fountain** (1923), depicting a fierce, watery battle between the two beasts. Not far away sits a bronze version of Denmark's favourite son, storyteller Hans Christian Andersen, near the boulevard that bears his name. It is on this busy road that you'll notice a very prominent feature of Danish life – the ubiquitous bicycle.

The road to the northwest of Rådhuspladsen is Vesterbrogade, which leads to Central Station, the **Copenhagen Visitor Centre** (see page 137) and Tivoli Gardens.

Tivoli Gardens

Across Hans Christian Andersens Boulevard from Rådhuspladsen is Copenhagen's most famous attraction, **Tivoli Gardens** ❷ (main entrance Vesterbrogade 3; www.tivoli.dk; charge).

Opened in 1843, this old-time pleasure park offers a joyous combination of theatrical performances, concerts, cafés and restaurants, and funfair rides and amusements, all set in beautiful gardens in the heart of the city. Visitors are welcomed by attendants dressed in old-fashioned outfits who embody a sense of dignity and tradition – qualities that infuse Tivoli. At the Pantomime Theatre, for instance, the mimed antics of Harlequin, Columbine and the clown Pierrot are accompanied not by pre-recorded music but by a small orchestra. The Tivoli Boys' Guard brass band frequently parades through the park, dressed in red-and-white uniforms and bearskin caps. Another 19th-century tradition is the fireworks display that begins and ends the opening season.

Night-time illuminations at Tivoli's pagoda

Rollercoaster Rides & Amusements

With its lake and lawns, water features and prolific flowerbeds, Tivoli fulfils its role as a traditional landscaped garden. Archaic side stalls, a traditional merry-go-round and a vintage trolleybus ride add to the feeling that you have stepped back into an older, gentler era. But it's not all coconut shies and hoopla – there are plenty of modern rides to set the pulse racing. Himmelskibet is one of the tallest carousels in the world, twirling its riders along at a height of 80m (262ft). The most extreme of the park's four rollercoasters is Dæmonen, which loops-the-loop at speeds of up to 80kph (50mph). Spinning amid the gears of a giant clock, Tik Tak, though not as fast, is at least as disorienting a ride.

> **NOTES**
>
> Tivoli throws open its doors for the festive season in the run-up to Christmas each year. The lake is frozen for skating and stalls offer tempting seasonal wares.

For kids, excitements include a classic carousel, soaring aeroplanes and miniature classic cars. For the even fainter of heart, the dragon boats on the lake have a romantic appeal. To go on any of the rides you'll need a ride pass (from 189kr) in addition to the entrance fee (from 160kr; or from 349km combined), valid all day. Prices do vary based on date so you can save by avoiding weekends and holidays.

Night-time Wonderland

As darkness falls, the atmosphere changes as thousands of multicoloured lights illuminate the park and its fairy-tale buildings, and music fills the air. The open-air stage is the focus for spectacular productions, such as *A Tivoli Fairy-tale* celebrating Hans Christian Andersen. On Friday evenings the Glassalen is the venue for pop and rock concerts featuring bands from Denmark and abroad. Jazz, blues and swing are all on the Tivoli programme. For classical music, check out the main Concert Hall, home of the Copenhagen Philharmonic (www.copenhagenphil.dk). Many of the performances are free.

Tivoli's 40 bars and restaurants are favourite meeting places for friends, families and businesspeople, and range from cafés to top-quality restaurants. It can be difficult to get a seat on warm summer evenings, so book ahead.

Vesterbro

Turn left out of the main Tivoli gate onto Vesterbrogade. The **Freedom Pillar** monument commemorates the end of serfdom in Denmark in 1788, and marks the start of Vesterbro, once a

Thrilling rides are all part of the fun at Tivoli

THE MAN WHO MADE TIVOLI

The driving force behind Tivoli was the 19th-century polyglot entrepreneur Georg Cartensen. He had travelled widely and seen the idea in practice in cities such as Paris. His vision was to combine a pleasure garden with venues for cultural events and a fair. But first he had to persuade the king, Christian VIII, of his plan's viability. The king gave his assent 'to provide the masses with suitable entertainment and fun', and Tivoli opened its doors to the public in August 1843. Crowds flocked to the gardens to see pantomimes, shows and fireworks displays and enjoy the rides, fairground stalls and concerts. Among the first attractions was a cable-car ride. Over the years, Tivoli has been modernised and extended, but its magic is undiminished, and it still retains a special place in the hearts of the Danes.

down-at-heel district known for its slaughterhouses and red-light area. Today it's on the up, with quirky boutiques and snug cafés. Some of the city's trendiest clubs and restaurants have moved into the former meat-packing sector **Kødbyen** ❸, making it one of the best places in town for evening entertainment – turn left down Colbjørnsensgade, then right onto Halmtorvet to find it.

No visit to Copenhagen is complete without sampling the local brew at the state-of-the-art **Home of Carlsberg** (Gammel Carlsbergvej 11, Valby; www.visitcarlsberg.com; charge), reopened after expensive renovations in 2023. Today's interactive museum occupies the grounds of the beer giant's first brewery, set right on the edge of Vesterbro – either meander through the district or hop on bus 8A or 26. Jacob Christian Jacobsen (1811–87), the brewery's founder, wanted to prove that industrial enterprises could be beautiful as well as functional, and so the whole site is surprisingly ornate. Gargoyles and lotus flowers decorate the Carlsberg chimney, while the Renaissance-style brew house is adorned with mosaics and sculptures. Jacob named his beer Carlsberg after his son,

Carl (1842–1914). But father and son did not see eye to eye and Carl eventually opened his own brewery next door. For those looking for more than the single pint included in the standard visit, there are also expert-led beer tasting tours in the brewery's historic cellars.

Strøget and Beyond

Highlights

- **Strøget**, see page 39
- **Around Kongens Nytorv**, see page 40
- **South of Strøget**, see page 42
- **Gammelstrand**, see page 44

Royal Copenhagen Porcelain

One of the first places you'll visit after Rådhuspladsen is Copenhagen's most famous pedestrian-only street. Known as **Strøget** ❹ (pronounced, roughly, stroy-et), this is a continuation of four streets – Frederiksberggade (leading off Rådhuspladsen), Nygade Vimmelskaftet, Amagertorv and Østergade – that wind their way for 1km (0.6 miles) to Kongens Nytorv (King's New Square). This traffic-free haven offers visitors an amazing assortment of shops, along with numerous small bars, restaurants, cafés and an abundance of street performers.

WHERE TO SHOOT THE BEST PICTURES

Rosenborg Slot

Inside and out, this red-brick Renaissance edifice decorated with spires and towers and ornate Dutch gables, offers wonderful photography opportunities. Head to the magnificent Knight's Hall, with its superb stucco ceiling and coronation chair. No tripods or selfie sticks allowed.

Our Saviour's Church

Capped by an iconic tower, Vor Frelsers Kirke is an unmissable feature of the Christianshavn skyline. Reached via a narrow staircase, the tower offers excellent views of the city and the countryside beyond.

Botanical Gardens

Packing in pretty much every plant you'll find in Denmark together with exotic species, these gardens are a nature photographer's dream.

Rådhus

Dominating the city's bustling cobbled main square, the grand Rådhus is a worthy picture subject as is the square itself.

Nyhavn

Arrive early to beat the crowds at the most photographed district in all of Copenhagen. The pastel-coloured merchants' houses lining this canal date back to its 17th-century construction.

Wander off Strøget to explore the small side streets: each of these has its own surprises among the numerous antiques shops, speciality stores, boutiques and fashionable restaurants.

Strøget

The entrance to Frederiksberggade, dominated by fast-food outlets, is not exactly prepossessing; however, perseverance will bring its rewards. Where Frederiksberggade ends, Strøget opens out into two squares on either side of the street. **Gammeltorv**, to the left, is a popular place for small market stalls and is home to the **Caritas Fountain** which, dating from 1610, is the city's oldest. In a tradition going back to the golden wedding of King Christian IX and Queen Louise in 1892, imitation golden apples are made to dance on the jets of the fountain on both Constitution Day (5 June) and the King's birthday (26 May). **Nytorv**, to the right, is dominated by the impressive architecture of the law courts. Each of these squares is a good place to sit at a street café and watch the procession of passing people.

The next place of note is the **Helligåndskirken** (Church of the Holy Spirit; www.helligaandskirken.dk). Built in the 17th–18th century, it is set in its own small gardens. Outside is an area particularly popular with street performers and other hawkers. Just past this point, Strøget opens out again and on the left side of Amagertorv you'll see a fine example of Dutch Baroque buildings – home to the group of **Royal Copenhagen** shops (see page 94). One of these, at No. 6, is the Royal Copenhagen Porcelain store, an Aladdin's cave with an elegant restaurant. It dates from 1616. Next door, Georg Jensen (www.georgjensen.com) features tableware sets designed over the last century. For the best of Danish design, pop into Illums Bolighus (www.illumsbolighus.com) at No. 10, an elegant department store featuring kitchenware, lighting and furniture.

As Amagertorv becomes Østergade, the shops become even more upmarket. Pause to look in the window of Halberstadt at No. 4 (www.halberstadt.com) – a jeweller founded in 1846 – which features a small golden train encrusted with diamonds and gems that runs continually around.

Around Kongens Nytorv

Kongens Nytorv ❺, the 'King's New Square' of Christian V – dating from 1680 and still the city's largest (12 streets lead off it) – is surrounded by impressive stately buildings. The park in the centre of the square is dominated by the king himself, in the form of an elaborate equestrian statue, with four classical figures seated submissively under his horse.

Kongens Nytorv, with the statue of Christian V

On the southwest side is the Old Stage of **Det Kongelige Teater** (Danish Royal Theatre; www.kglteater.dk). Founded in 1748, it briefly served as a stage for a 14-year-old Hans Christian Andersen, who tried without success to become a ballet dancer. This venerable building, the spiritual home of Denmark's national ballet, opera and theatre, has now relinquished many of its performances to a pair of state-of-the-art venues: the Royal Danish Playhouse (Skuespilhuset; Skt Annæ Plads) and, facing it across the water, the Opera House (Operaen; see page 73).

Next to the theatre stands **Charlottenborg Slot**, the oldest building on the square. It was built as a royal palace in 1683 in the style of Dutch baroque and, since 1754, has been the home of the Royal Danish Academy of Fine Arts. Enter through the front gate and at the rear is **Kunsthal Charlottenborg**, which exhibits Danish and international contemporary art (www.kunsthalcharlottenborg.dk; free).

Look around the square and you will notice other splendid buildings. **Thotts Palae** (Thott's Mansion), in the northeast corner, was built for the naval hero Admiral Niels Juel and is now home to the French Embassy. Not to be outdone is the wonderful facade of the **Hotel d'Angleterre** (www.dangleterre.com), one of Denmark's finest hotels.

The unusually shaped building on the corner of Nyhavn (see page 60), tucked between Store Strandstræde and Bredgade, is the beautifully preserved 1782 **Kanneworffs Hus**, which houses the jewellery shop House of Amber and a small **Amber Museum** (www.houseofamber.com; free). Diagonally across the square is the imposing seven-storey **Magasin du Nord** (www.magasin.dk), Scandinavia's first department store.

South of Strøget

Leave Kongens Nytorv by Vingårdsstræde at the southwest corner of Magasin du Nord. You'll find yourself in an area of jazz clubs, small bars and artists' hang-outs. At its junction with Admiralgade is the massive 70m (230ft) tall copper spire of **Skt Nicolai Kirke** (St Nicholas Church). Destroyed several times by fire and rebuilt as recently as 1917, it houses the **Nikolaj Kunsthal** (www.nikolajkunsthal.dk; charge; free entry Wed), which has a small permanent collection and an innovative programme of temporary exhibitions. At the south end of Admiralgade is **Holmens Kirke** (www.holmenskirke.dk; free). The church is in the Venetian style, but with Dutch gable ends and a small copper tower in the middle. The building was originally a 16th-century anchor forge, but was transformed in 1619 by Christian IV into a sailors' church. On the altar, reredos and pulpit there is a profusion of oak carvings by Abel Schrøder the Younger. Look for the votive ship hanging from the ceiling, a tradition common in many Danish churches.

Holmens Kirke, the sailors' church

Outside Holmens Kirke you are now by the canal, and it is impossible not to be impressed by the Christiansborg complex on the opposite bank (see page 46). Turn right up Ved Stranden and head for the Højbro bridge and the junction with Gammelstrand and Højbro Plads.

Within a short distance of here are three very different statues. The most obvious of these, on **Højbro Plads**, is the magnificent copper green **equestrian statue of Bishop Absalon** showing the warrior-priest in chain mail with axe in hand. On the corner of Gammelstrand stands the **statue of the Fiskerkone** (Fisherman's Wife), scarf on her head, shawl around her shoulders, wearing an apron and clasping a fish. Erected in 1940, she resembles the women who for centuries sold fish along the wharf. The third sculpture is less obvious; in fact, you'll have to look over the bridge to discover the submerged legend of the **'Merman with Seven Sons'**, who appeal to their human mother Agnete to return to them.

Gammelstrand

Next, turn into Gammelstrand itself; the name means 'old beach' and, as this implies, it is the former edge of the city. This is one of the two principal starting points for canal-boat tours, the other being in Nyhavn (see page 60). Immediately across the canal lies a distinctive square-arched, yellow-ochre building with a classical-style frieze, looking like a national tomb: a monument to the great Danish sculptor Bertel Thorvaldsen (1770–1844; see page 50). Off to the right, on Frederiksholms Kanal, you'll be able to make out the arched entrance to the colossal Nationalmuseet (see page 52). Gammelstrand also has restaurants and bars, among which is the elegant **Krogs** seafood restaurant (http://krogs.dk).

Time now to proceed back to Rådhuspladsen, via a collection of interesting old streets. At the western end of Gammelstrand, Snaregade features some timber-framed houses. Continue into Magstræde, where the houses at numbers 17 and 19 are two of the city's oldest, dating from 1640. Next is **Vandkunsten**, a delightful little square with outdoor cafés and a fountain on the spot where the city's first water pipes were laid. Continue across the next junction into Gåsegade, and look for the gabled houses with 18th-century hoists at the top. Furniture is traditionally hauled up by these hoists, rather than being

NOTES

Holmens Kirke remains a favourite with the royal family. In 1967 Queen Margrethe (r. 1972–2024) was married here to Prince Henrik (formerly the French Count de Laborde de Monpezat). It's also the resting place of her father, King Frederik IX (1947–1972), grandfather of the currently reigning King Frederik X.

squeezed up the narrow stairwells.

On the corner of Hestemøllestræde and Lavendelstræde is a house where Mozart's widow lived with her second husband, a Danish diplomat. Here, the huge archways of Copenhagen's fourth town hall dominate; built between 1805 and 1815, it now houses the law courts. On Lavendelstræde you'll find typical Danish houses and shops from 1796, the year after the city's second great fire, and at the end of the street Vester Voldgade leads to Rådhuspladsen.

Vandkunsten square

On and Around Slotsholmen

Highlights

- **Christiansborg and its Museums**, see page 46
- **National Museum 44**, see page 52
- **Museum of Copenhagen**, see page 53
- **Ny Carlsberg Glyptotek**, see page 54

Starting at Rådhuspladsen, retrace your steps on the previous tour back to the Højbro bridge and then cross it to the small island of Slotsholmen (Castle Island) and the imposing towers of Christiansborg. A little further along the canal is one of the

> **NOTES**
>
> Give your feet a rest with a trip on the harbour bus, which connects the Royal Library's Black Diamond building with the Little Mermaid, stopping at Holmen, Nyhavn and the Opera House en route.

city's best-known landmarks, **Børsen** ❻ (the Stock Exchange). After 400 years as a city landmark, most of the building went up in flames in April of 2024, including its eye-catching spire composed of four entwined dragons' tails. Just five months after the fire that laid waste to the historic Stock Exchange, King Frederik laid the first stone of building's reconstruction. To stay more or less true to the original 17th-century design, it will require the shipping of 800,000 stone blocks, traditionally manufactured, and 800 large pines from Germany for its timber roof. When the fire broke out, the active Stock Exchange had long since emigrated to Strøget, but it's expected that the new construction's thoroughly modernized facilities will see it return to regular community use upon its eventual completion – which is currently slated for 2028. Check online for details.

Christiansborg and its Museums

Christiansborg ❼ (www.christiansborgslot.dk; charge) is the fifth castle or palace to have stood on this site since Absalon built his fortress in 1167: pillage, fire and rebuilding frenzies have taken their toll on the earlier ones. The second castle became the permanent seat of the king and government in 1417. The present edifice dates from the early 20th century, at which time Thorvald Jørgensen won an architectural competition for the design of a new Christiansborg palace. On 15 November 1907, King Frederik VIII laid the cornerstone that had been hewn out of the granite remains from Absalon's original castle. Above this a vast plinth was made of 7,500 boulders donated by 750 Danish boroughs, and then the palace was faced with granite slabs. Look up to see 57 granite masks of Denmark's greatest men. Covered in copper between 1937 and 1939, the roof of Christiansborg makes an imposing addition to the city's verdigris skyline.

The chapel, theatre museum, riding stables and beautifully restored **Marmorbroen** (Marble Bridge), which survived two disastrous fires in 1794 and 1884, help to give the palace a more venerable aspect than its more recent origins suggest. Today the castle (nicknamed 'Borgen', as in the name of the award-winning Danish political TV series) houses government ministries, Parliament (Folketing) and the Danish Supreme Court, as well as being the centre of a complex of museums.

Christiansborg, seat of the Danish Parliament

DANISH THRILLER

Across Scandinavia, Nordic Noir has hit the big time. Although Denmark hasn't (yet) produced a popular crime writer with the stature of a Henning Mankell, Stieg Larsson or Jo Nesbø, it has made a huge impact in TV terms. From the moment detective Sarah Lund stepped into the frame in *The Killing* (*Forbrydelsen*; 2007), viewers were hooked. The equally addictive *Borgen* (2010) followed, about a politician, Birgitte Nyborg, who becomes the first female prime minister of Denmark. Then came *The Bridge* (*Broen*; 2011), which begins in suitably grisly fashion with the discovery of a bisected corpse on the Øresund Bridge, half lying in Denmark and half in Sweden… All three series went on to have two sequels each and both *The Killing* and *The Bridge* were adapted in other countries. Location tours are available with **Nordic Noir Tours** (http://nordicnoirtours.com; by reservation only, starting from Vesterport Station).

The most notable highlights of the complex include the **Kongelige Repræsentationslokaler** (Royal Reception Rooms; guided tours in English daily 3pm, in July–Aug also at noon; charge). One of the guide's first anecdotes will probably be: 'Look at the roof here, held by pillars in the shape of male statues, heads bent to take the weight – a symbol of modern Danes paying their taxes…' You can also visit the Reception Rooms on your own.

The Reception Rooms, on the first floor, are used by the King and Prime Minister for official receptions, state banquets, and royal audiences with foreign ambassadors. They are richly decorated with works of art retrieved from the earlier palaces, as well as pieces by modern Danish artists. Most impressive is the 40m (130ft) long Great Hall hung with a series of tapestries by Bjørn Nørgaard recounting the history of Denmark. They were a 50th birthday present for Queen Margrethe II. Made by Les Gobelins in Paris, they took 10 years to complete. Other chambers include the Throne Room and the balcony overlooking Slotspladsen (Castle

Square), from where monarchs are proclaimed. It's also here that the King receives his birthday congratulations (26th of May), cheered by the crowds that fill the square below.

In the palace basement you will find the **Ruinerne af Absalons Borg** (Ruins of Absalon's Palace; charge) from 1167, as well as remnants of more recent castles on the site. Also in the complex is the **Folketing** (Danish Parliament; www.thedanishparliament.dk; guided tours in English every Fri at 10am year round, bookings via the website; free).

Out in the vast parade ground, dominated by a copper equestrian statue of Christian IX, are the **Kongelige Stalde og Kareter** (Royal Stables; charge). The stables are home to some fine driving

A royal carriage on display in Christiansborg's stables

and riding horses, which can sometimes be seen exercising in the square. On display are uniforms and royal state carriages dating from 1778.

Theatre Museum

In an elegant terrace above the stables is the **Teatermuseet** (Theatre Museum; www.teatermuseet.dk; charge), a small museum adjoining a theatre built exclusively for the court in 1767. The delightful little auditorium and galleries are packed with costumes, set models and other theatrical relics.

Thorvaldsens Museum

Throngs of painted people decorate the ochre facade of **Thorvaldsens Museum** ❽ (thorvaldsensmuseum.dk; closed Mon; charge), on the Gammelstrand side of Christiansborg. The museum is dedicated to the celebrated Danish sculptor Bertel Thorvaldsen (1770–1844) who, at the tender age of 11, was accepted into the Copenhagen Art Academy. Later he won a scholarship to Rome, where he lived and worked for more than 40 years. On his triumphant return to Denmark, he chose a young architect, Gottlieb Bindesbøll, to design a museum to house his sculptures. The result is one of Copenhagen's most distinctive buildings, both inside and out, its richly coloured walls contrasting with the pure white plaster and marble of Thorvaldsen's sculptures.

Danish War Museum

In a side street behind the Royal Stables, **Krigsmuseet** (Danish War Museum, Tøjhusgade 3; https://natmus.dk; charge) holds a fascinating collection of military items, including an early 15th-century cannon from the time of Queen Margrete I and modern weapons. Cannonballs are piled high like potatoes and old military planes are suspended from the roof. The revamped Armoury Hall on the first floor houses a permanent exhibition about Denmark's bellicose past. The museum also presents the history and development of the Danish Navy.

Royal Library

Close by are the **Royal Library Gardens** (daily 6am–10pm), an oasis of peace and calm designed in 1920. Built in 1906, the grand building facing the gardens is the former Royal Library, of which the earliest iteration here was built in 1648 by Frederik III. On its left side you won't miss the angular entrance to the **Dansk Jødisk Museum** (Danish Jewish Museum; Proviantpassagen 6; www.jewmus.dk; charge). A masterpiece of modern design by eminent architect Daniel Libeskind, it stands on the site of Christian IV's Royal Galley House and was extensively renovated before reopening in 2022. Multi-sensory displays inside tell the tumultuous story of Denmark's Jews, down to the heroic rescue efforts of Danes during the Nazi occupation.

The tranquil gardens of the Royal Library

Walk around the building to the waterfront and be prepared for an architectural surprise on an even grander scale. On Søren Kierkegaards Plads a seven-storey, glass, granite, concrete and steel structure appears to be leaning towards the river. This, because of its colour, is called **Den Sorte Diamant** (The Black Diamond), serving as the new location of **Det Kongelige Bibliotek** (Royal Library; www.kb.dk; tours Mon 3pm year-round and Sat 1pm July and Aug;

free). Since opening in 1999, it has also hosted concerts, lectures and meetings, and is home to a lovely restaurant and café overlooking the water.

From Søren Kierkegaards Plads walk across the river, along Christians Brygge, until you see the landmark building of **BLOX** (blox.dk) on Bryghuspladsen, on the Copenhagen harbour front. Designed by the internationally-acclaimed OMA firm, it was inaugurated in 2018 and houses, along with several other institutions, the **Dansk Arkitektur Center** (Danish Architecture Centre; www.dac.dk; charge), which hosts workshops, lectures and some excellent exhibitions, including a permanent gallery devoted to Danish architecture through the ages. Entitled 'So Danish!', this exhibition was launched in celebration of the city's designation as UNESCO's World Capital of Architecture in 2023.

National Museum

From BLOX, follow Frederiksholms Kanal to the north, turning left on Ny Vestergade to reach the **Nationalmuseet** ❾ (National Museum; www.natmus.dk; charge). Denmark's largest museum, it focuses mainly on Danish history from the Stone Age to modern times. A definite highlight of its trove of prehistoric displays is the Trundholm Sun Chariot (1200 BC), dating from a period when the Danes worshipped the sun, imagining it as a disc of gold riding through the sky in a chariot behind a celestial horse. Subsequent eras are reflected in collections of altarpieces, coinage, armour and Renaissance art. Other sections of the museum

NOTES

The word *mitzvah* on the door of the Danish Jewish Museum means 'a good deed'. It relates to the remarkable rescue in 1943 of 7,000 Jews who, in the face of deportation to Nazi concentration camps, were hidden and taken in small boats to Sweden.

The elaborate Glyptoteket gallery

contain ethnographic exhibits from around the world, offering fascinating glimpses of the Danish colonial experience in Greenland, West Africa and the West Indies. There's also a wonderful collection of classical and Near Eastern artefacts, among them Greek sculpture, Persian pottery and mummies, while a hands-on Children's Museum provides an interesting diversion for youngsters.

Museum of Copenhagen

Kitty-corner to the west of Nationalmuseet is the small but excellent **Københavns Museum** (Museum of Copenhagen; Stormgade 18; www.cphmuseum.kk.dk; charge). First opened in the attic of City Hall in 1901, it was reopened a block to the east in its current location in 2020, now filling a beautifully restored, four-storey building. As well as a sweeping account of the city's brushes with wars, plague and social upheaval, the museum offers an intimate glimpse into the lives of Copenhageners past and present, from its earliest settlers to 20th-century shopkeepers, making the most of multisensory displays. Among the definite highlights is a large, interactive model of the city's historic core, making the museum an excellent stop to help you get your bearings.

Ny Carlsberg Glyptotek

Continue for a block down Stormgade and cross over Hans Christian Andersens Boulevard to reach the distinctively classical, dome-capped building which houses the **Ny Carlsberg Glyptotek** ⑩ (Dantes Plads 7; www.glyptoteket.com; charge). The Glyptotek was founded on the classical collection of Carl Jacobsen (1842–1914), a Danish brewer and art connoisseur. Under its elaborate roof lies one of the world's foremost displays of Egyptian, Greek, Roman and Etruscan art. The sub-tropical garden in its central hall appears to have been transplanted directly from ancient Rome. In contrast, the French collection – works by Gauguin, van Gogh and Monet, Rodin sculptures and a complete set of Degas bronzes – is in a glorious modern wing, built in 1996 and designed by Henning Larsen (creator of Copenhagen's Opera House).

University Quarter and Parks

Highlights

- **Copenhagen Cathedral**, see page 55
- **University and Gråbrødretorv**, see page 56
- **Round Tower**, see page 56
- **Rosenborg Slot**, see page 57
- **Fine Arts Museum**, see page 59

From Rådhuspladsen, go northwest for a short way along Vester Voldgade and then turn right into narrow Studiestræde, home to a melange of antiques shops, bookstalls and boutiques gathered in an 18th-century setting.

At Studiestræde 6 a plaque records that H.C. Ørsted, who discovered electro-magnetism in 1820, lived here. A few metres further on, at the corner of Nørregade, is one of Copenhagen's oldest preserved buildings, the former Bispegården (Bishop's Residence), built in 1500 and part of the university. Nearby on Bispetorvet, a 1943 monument commemorates the 400th anniversary of the introduction of the Reformation to Denmark.

Copenhagen Cathedral

At the end of Studiestræde stands the **Domkirke** ⓫ (Cathedral) of Copenhagen, known as **Vor Frue Kirke** (Church of Our Lady; www.domkirken.dk; free). Bishop Absalon's successor, Sunesen, is said to have laid its foundations in the 12th century, but by 1316 it had already burned down four times. Later, two further constructions were destroyed – by the great 1728 fire and by British bombardment in 1807. The present church was reconstructed by V.F.K. and C.F. Hansen between 1811 and 1829. Its austere interior balanced by a collection of heroic statues by Bertel Thorvaldsen: 12 massive marble Apostles line the

Picturesque Gråbrødretorv

aisle, while an orange-lit altar is surrounded by bronze candelabra and dominated by his figure of Christ. Thorvaldsen's statue of Christ in Vor Frue Kirke, known as the Christus (*Kristus*), has inspired faithful replicas around the world, particularly among members of the Mormon Church (the Church of Jesus Christ of Latter-Day Saints), for whom its likeness has served as an official logo since 2020.

University and Gråbrødretorv

Proceed along the north side of the Cathedral. On the left is the main Copenhagen University block, which dates back in its present form only as far as the 1830s. The university was founded in 1479. This is a typical student area with a number of interesting bookshops and cafés.

A spiral ramp winds around the inside of the Round Tower

Turn right into Fiolstræde, a lively spot for alfresco dining, and left into Skindergade, which leads into **Gråbrødretorv** (Greyfriar's Square), a large, picturesque traffic-free square surrounded by brightly painted 18th-century houses. Now ringed with cafés and restaurants, it was the site of a Franciscan monastery until the Reformation.

Round Tower

Continue along Skindergade to Købmagergade and you'll find yourself at the foot of one of Copenhagen's most beloved landmarks, the **Rundetaarn** ⓬ (Round Tower; www.rundetaarn.dk; charge). The Round Tower was built by Christian IV in 1642 as part of his vision to provide an astronomical observatory, church and university library for 17th-century scholars. You can walk to the top of the 36m (118ft) high tower, but not by any ordinary means – steps would have been impractical for raising the heavy equipment needed here. Instead, a wide spiral ramp, 210m (690ft) long, winds around inside the tower. Not only did Tsar Peter the Great ride up to the top on horseback in 1716, but his empress followed him in a horse-drawn coach. You can see the core of tower looking down from a glass floor and there is a splendid view over the rooftops of the old city from the top. **Trinitatis Kirke** (Trinity Church) is to the rear of the tower; look through the glass panel in the wall at the bottom of the ramp. The library hall above is now used for exhibitions and concerts.

> **NOTES**
>
> The Rundetaarn (Round Tower) has the oldest functioning observatory in Europe. If you happen to be here in winter, you can view the night sky through its telescope (www.rundetaarn.dk).

The building across Købmagergade from the Round Tower, at the corner with Krystalgade, is the Regensen university hostel. Although students have lived here since 1623, most of the present structure dates from the 18th century. A couple of hundred metres along Krystalgade stands the Synagogue of Copenhagen (www.mosaiske.dk; daily guided tours June–Aug, charge), inaugurated in 1833.

Rosenborg Slot

Backtrack to the Round Tower and turn right, following Landemærket to its end at Copenhagen's favourite park, **Kongens**

Have (King's Garden), filled with sunbathers, picnickers and families in summer. This garden was laid out in 1606–34 by Christian IV, who found Christiansborg Palace too official and oppressive. He built himself a small country mansion in a corner of the site, outside the town walls, eventually expanding it into the three-storey Dutch Renaissance-style **Rosenborg Slot** ⓭ (Rosenborg Castle; www.kongernessamling.dk; charge). Rosenborg became home for the next three generations of kings until Frederik IV erected Frederiksberg Castle in 1710. Since 1838 it has been a royal museum of considerable grace and the home of the crown jewels.

The castle's rooms are arranged chronologically, beginning with Christian IV's tower-room study, still furnished in its original style. The Knights' Hall, with tapestries depicting Danish victories in the Swedish Wars, an ornate ceiling and three almost life-size silver lions, contains one of the world's largest collections of silver furniture, mostly from the 18th century.

The crown jewels are held in the treasury. In addition to the oldest existing insignia of the Order of the Elephant (see box), there are 18 cases of crowns, gilded swords, precious stones and coronation cups – as well as silver boxes containing the umbilical cords of eight royal children. The centrepiece of this regal collection is the 17th-century crown of the absolute monarchy – made out of gold, diamonds, sapphires and garnets and weighing over 2kg (4lbs).

Also not to be missed is the nearby **David Collection** ⓮ (Kronprincessegade 30; www.davidmus.dk; free), which has outstanding collections of European and Islamic fine art, the latter's exhibits spanning from Arab-ruled Andalucia to Mughal India.

On the other side of Rosenborg, across Øster Voldgade, spreads the **Botanisk Have** ⓯ (Botanical Gardens; snm.dk; gardens: free; palm house: charge: combined ticket with museum). Born in its current location in 1870, it hosts Denmark's largest collection of living plants. Near the garden's centre, the Victorian-style, glass-enclosed Palm House has stood since 1874, sheltering the garden's tropical

Formal gardens around Rosenborg Slot

species. A spiral, cast-iron staircase inside climbs 16m to afford wonderful views over the canopy. The combined zoological, botanical and geological collections of the city are being merged into one stunning new **Natural History Museum of Denmark** (www.snm.dk; charge: combined ticket with Palm House), to open in 2026 at the block's northern corner, promising to showcase some 14 million items. Until then, the old museum location to the south – though comparably modest – remains open and worthwhile.

Fine Arts Museum

Art lovers should allow themselves time to explore the **Statens Museum for Kunst** ⓰ (National Gallery of Denmark; Sølvgade 48–50; www.smk.dk; charge), just north of the Botanical Gardens. Paintings from early Dutch to modern Danish, including a large

NOTES

The Order of the Elephant is Denmark's highest decoration. Instituted by Christian V in 1693, the insignia is worn by members of the royal family and can be bestowed upon foreign heads of state. As was his mother Queen Elizabeth II, Britain's King Charles III is a member of the Order.

Matisse collection and perhaps the world's finest collection of Dürer prints, are housed in a light, airy and beautifully renovated building.

Across the park at Stockholmsgade 20 is **Den Hirschsprungske Samling** (Hirschsprung Collection; www.hirschsprung.dk; charge), a delightful museum packed with 19th-century Danish painting, sculpture and decorative art. Heinrich Hirschsprung, a tobacco merchant, donated the works to the state in 1902. Look out for the portraits and landscapes of C.W. Eckersberg (1783–1853), whose meticulous style had a far-reaching influence.

It's possible to return to Rådhuspladsen by bus or by train from Nørreport Station. But, if you prefer to walk, another surprise awaits: the leafy **Ørsteds Parken**, on the right-hand side of Nørre Voldgade. Wrapped around a little lake, this charming park offers a wonderful respite during daylight hours.

Nyhavn and Beyond

Highlights

- **Amaliehavn Gardens**, see page 62
- **Amalienborg Palace**, see page 62
- **Churchill Park**, see page 65
- **The Little Mermaid**, see page 66
- **The Citadel**, see page 66
- **A Stroll along Bredgade**, see page 68
- **Marble Church**, see page 69

This walk begins at Kongens Nytorv (bus 26 from Rådhuspladsen). Cross the square towards **Nyhavn** ⓱; the name literally means 'new harbour' and immediately you'll notice the nautical flavour of this former 'sailors' street', once overflowing with bars and brothels. Over the centuries the two sides of the canal have developed into a remarkable illustration of old Copenhagen. At the Kongens Nytorv end of the canal, which was dug in 1671 to enlarge the harbour, stands a sizeable old anchor, a memorial to the Danish sailors killed in World War II. On either side of the canal itself, an unusual collection of vessels lies at anchor with their masts colourfully bedecked with the Danish flag. This sight, combined with numerous restaurants and bars with outside terraces, and the antiques

Colourful Nyhavn

shops and other stores on the north side, draws thousands of people who are only too happy to eat, drink and socialise in such an attractive and lively setting.

This is a street with everything – history, architecture, nightlife and a constant passage of small, colourful vessels. It was even home to Hans Christian Andersen, who lived here first at number 67 from 1854–64 and later at number 18.

Walk to the end of Nyhavn on the north side (with all the cafés), and you'll pass Nyhavn 71 (www.71nyhavnhotel.com), a superb hotel conversion of an 18th-century warehouse. Just beyond is a view over the inner harbour to the Christianshavn area, where the spiralling steeple of Vor Frelsers Kirke dominates the skyline (see page 71).

Amaliehavn Gardens

Turn left down Toldbodgade to Skt Annæ Plads. This is a fine boulevard lined with consulates and distinguished old offices, with an equestrian statue of Christian X at the end overlooking Bredgade. To your right is the **Royal Danish Playhouse** ⓲ (Skuespilhuset; https://kglteater.dk). Cross the square, turn right and then left along the waterfront to the pleasant **Amaliehavn Gardens**. These were created by Belgian landscape architect Jean Delogne in 1983 using French limestone and Danish granite. The bronze pillars around the fountain were designed by Italian sculptor Arnaldo Pomodoro. Across the water you'll see the magnificent Opera House (see page 73).

Amalienborg Palace

The road leading away from the water takes you to one of the most attractively symmetrical squares in Europe, **Amalienborg Plads**. A huge equestrian statue of Frederik V, 21 years in the making, dominates the centre of the square and gives you a clue that you are now in the proximity of royalty. The four (superficially) identical mansions that line the octagonal perimeter were designed by superstar 18th-century architect Nicolai Eigtved as town mansions for four noblemen. After Christiansborg Palace was destroyed by fire in 1794, the homeless royal family purchased the mansions from their aristocratic owners, and has lived here since. Today, collectively known as **Amalienborg Slot** ⓳ (Palace), these buildings are considered among the finest rococo ensembles in all of Europe.

Four roads converge at right angles on the courtyard, while bearskin-clad soldiers guard each of the palaces and corners, with an extra sentry posted at the gateway between the two palaces to your left. The wing to the left of the colonnade is Christian IX's Palace, which has remained the winter residence of Queen Margrethe

Amalienborg Plads and Palace, home of the royal family

since her abdication. On the right of the colonnade, **Christian VII's Palace** is used for receptions and to house royal guests.

Continuing around the square, the third building, Christian VIII's Palace, houses the **Amalienborg Palace Museum** (www.kongernessamling.dk; charge), where the Royal Collection is on show in the splendid private apartments of the Danish Glücksburg kings. Among the exhibits are treasured works of art given to Christian IX (reigned 1863–1906) and Queen Louise by their six children, some of whom married into other leading European royal families. The fourth building is Frederik VIII's Palace, home to King Frederik, Queen Mary and their children. The name Amalienborg came from the wife of Frederik III, Queen Sophie Amalie.

Majestic Marmorkirken (the Marble Church)

The main attraction at Amalienborg when the Queen is in residence is the daily **Changing of the Guard**. At 11.27am the guards leave their barracks near Rosenborg Castle (see page 57) in formation, and march through the city streets so as to arrive in the palace square just before noon, moving from one sentry box to another in a series of foot-stamping ceremonies. Guardsmen march to the accompaniment of a band, their black bearskins rippling in the breeze. They wear blue trousers with white stripes and highly polished boots; on festive occasions they dress in red tunics with white shoulder straps.

Churchill Park

Leave the square via Amaliegade and follow it north for about 730m/yards to its junction with Esplanaden. Churchill Parken is on the opposite side of the road and has several interesting sights.

Frihedsmuseet ⓴ (Museum of the Danish Resistance 1940–45; www.natmus.dk; charge) enjoys a gorgeous location, especially in springtime when the daffodils are in bloom. In contrast, the museum provides a nuanced record of the wartime struggle against the German occupation. Founded in 1957 by members of the Resistance Movement, the museum burned down in 2013, reopening its doors in 2020 with a fresh, interactive layout that takes in the era through the eyes of real people who were present here, among them local members of both the Resistance and counter-resistance.

Just beyond, the Anglican **St Alban's Church** (free) looks as if it has been transplanted from an English country village. It was indeed constructed amid the green lawns of Churchill Park in 1887 by an English architect. On a small slope next to the church there is a sight that is guaranteed to hold your attention. Copenhagen has numerous fountains but this, the **Gefion Fountain**, is the most spectacular. Commissioned by the Carlsberg Foundation and placed here in 1908, the sculpture is Anders Bundgaard's

All quiet at the Citadel

depiction of the legend of the Nordic goddess Gefion – who turned her four sons into oxen and used them to pull the island of Zealand from Sweden.

The Little Mermaid

Follow the right-hand path through delightful gardens past the fountain and walk much further on to Langelinie (a waterside pier/promenade). Located just before the marina and the cruise-ship dock, near the water's edge, is Denmark's most famous statue, **Den Lille Havfrue** ㉑ (the Little Mermaid). In Andersen's fairy tale, this tragic sea-girl exchanged her voice for human legs in order to gain the love of an earthly prince, only to watch in silence as he jilted her for a human princess. In desperation, she threw herself into the sea and turned into foam. Unveiled in 1913, the mermaid's statue has been vandalized repeatedly since the 1960s, defaced, doused with paint, knocked over, had an arm sawn off – even decapitated twice. Fortunately, the workshop of sculptor Edvard Eriksen retains the original moulds, allowing for new parts to be cast when necessary.

The Citadel

After viewing the Little Mermaid, take the road running inland from the water, cross a bridge and descend the flight of steps on the left. This leads to a wooden bridge on the far side of which is **Kastellet** ㉒ (Citadel; free), a star-shaped fortress with five bastions, begun by Frederik III in 1662. Building continued until 1725 and today the fortress is still in use by the army – the church, prison and main guardhouse having resisted the assaults of time. It is a delightfully peaceful enclave, with a charming windmill (1847) and some remains of the old ramparts well worth seeing.

Leave by the wooden bridge leading south into Churchill Parken, then turn right onto Esplanaden. Cross Store Kongensgade into Gernersgade and you are in the heart of **Nyboder** ㉓ (New Dwellings), whose long rows of houses were first built between 1631 and 1641 by Christian IV as dwellings for his sailors. More

Twentieth-century design icons, Designmuseum Danmark

houses were built in the 18th and 19th centuries. Painted yellow-ochre, with steep gabled roofs and shuttered windows, they form a fashionable, well-preserved community of homes still inhabited by navy personnel as well as civilians. You can see what life here used to be like at **Nyboders Mindestuer** (St Pauls Gade 24; http://nybodersmindestuer.dk; charge), a small museum based in the cramped rooms of two 17th-century houses.

A Stroll along Bredgade

Backtrack to Bredgade and turn right. The area from here to Kongens Nytorv is a residential quarter of substantial granite houses and quadrangles. It was planned by architect Nicolai

The grandiose Marble Church, modelled on St Peter's in Rome

SØREN KIERKEGAARD

The top-hatted figure of Søren Kierkegaard (1813–55) was a familiar sight to Copenhageners as he took his daily walk along the city's cobbled streets. Regarded as one of the founders of Existentialism, Kierkegaard's philosophy developed out of personal anguish and his distaste for organised religion. Kierkegaard's fans can pay their respects at his resting place in Nørrebro's Assistens Cemetery. There's also a small exhibition devoted to the man at Københavns Museum (Museum of Copenhagen; https://cphmuseum.kk.dk).

Eigtved at about the same time as Amalienborg. At number 68 you'll find **Designmuseum Danmark** (http://designmuseum.dk; closed Mon; charge). Housed in an attractive rococo building (a former hospital) dating from 1757, the museum focuses on Danish and European decorative art, from patterned textiles and silverwares to pocket watches and porcelain figurines.

On one side of the museum, at number 70, there is a plaque commemorating the death of the philosopher Søren Kierkegaard (see box) in 1855. On the other side, at number 64, is Skt Ansgars Kirke, centre of the modest Roman Catholic community since 1842. A museum documents the history of Catholicism in the city since its virtual extinction in the Reformation of 1536. Immediately after the church stands the **Medicinsk Museion** (Bredgade 62; www.museion.ku.dk; charge) – the squeamish may shy away from its fascinating collection of medical artefacts, past and present, among them dissected body parts and pairs of conjoined twins encased in glass. Across the road from here are the golden onion-shaped domes of Alexander Nevsky Kirke, built for the Russian Orthodox community in 1883.

Marble Church

A few steps further and the great dome of the **Marmorkirken** **24** (Marble Church; www.marmorkirken.dk; church: free; dome: charge;

The new Opera House at Holmen

visits to the dome Sat and Sun 1pm), officially called the Frederiks Kirken, rises high to your right. Measuring 31m (100ft) in diameter, this is one of the largest church domes in Europe. The cornerstone was laid by Frederik V in 1749. However, the Norwegian marble required for the building became so expensive that the project was halted. It was eventually completed using Danish marble and consecrated in 1894.

Inside, the dome is decorated with rich frescoes in blue, gold and green, representing the Apostles. Outside, the building is surrounded by statues of personalities of the Danish Church, including St Ansgar, who helped to bring Christianity to Denmark, and Grundtvig, the 19th-century educationalist. On the roof are 16 religious figures, from Moses to Luther. Continue along Bredgade to Kongens Nytorv past an array of boutiques, antiques shops and galleries.

Christianshavn and Holmen

Highlights

- **Christians Kirke**, see page 71
- **Vor Frelsers Kirke**, see page 71
- **Christiania**, see page 73
- **Opera House**, see page 73

Though there's so much to see within a small radius of Rådhuspladsen and Kongens Nytorv, it's worth spending a few hours across the Knippelsbro bridge in **Christianshavn**. The area was named Christian's Harbour after Christian IV, and it looks like a slice of Amsterdam, reflecting the king's predilection for Dutch architecture.

Christians Kirke

Having crossed Knippel Bridge you are on Torvegade. Turn right at the intersection with Strandgade and stroll to the sombre **Christians Kirke** ㉕ (www.christianskirke.dk; free). Built in 1755 by Nicolai Eigtved, it possesses an unexpected interior layout with three tiers of galleries reminiscent of an old-time music hall. The tower was added in 1769.

Backtracking along Strandgade, continue until you reach Gammel Dok, the impressive former warehouse housing the Danish Art Workshops where artists can carry out their projects at special studios and workshops. The area has numerous 17th- and 18th-century houses with cobbled courtyards. N.F.S. Grundtvig spent some years at number 4B. Living at number 6 in the early 18th century was Admiral Peter Wessel Tordenskjold a Danish Norwegian hero who won battles at sea, but whose exuberant lifestyle ashore lost him many good neighbours. It's said that every time he called *skål* (cheers) during his frequent banquets, a salute would be fired from two cannons at the main doorway, with many a sleepless night had by all until his death in a duel in 1720.

Vor Frelsers Kirke

Follow Skt Annæ Gade from Strandgade towards the distinctive twisted spire of **Vor Frelsers Kirke** ㉖ (Church of Our Saviour; vorfrelserskirke.dk; church: free; tower: charge), consecrated in 1696. Its most dominant exterior feature, the dizzying staircase that twists four times around the creaking wooden tower, was designed by Lauridz de Thurah and completed in 1752. An eye-watering total of 400 steps, 150 on the outside, lead from the entrance of the church to the gilt globe and Christ figure on top of the spire.

Inside, the church's highlights include its choir screen, guarded by six wooden angels; the ornate white marble font supported by four cherubs; the altar dating from 1732, replete with allegorical statues and Dresden-like figures playing in the clouds; the tinkling carillon; and in particular the monumental organ, built in 1700 and several times remodelled, most recently in 1965. Beautifully ornamented, the whole construction is supported by two large stucco elephants.

Copenhagen rooftops from Vor Frelsers Kirke

Christiania

A spiral staircase surrounds Vor Frelsers Kirke tower

Outside Vor Frelsers Kirke, turn left onto Prinsessegade and follow the brick wall to a somewhat more esoteric experience. In 1971, a group of local people broke into an abandoned military barracks here and founded **Christiania** 27 free state. Denmark proclaimed it a social experiment soon thereafter, and it has provoked controversy ever since. For many years, soft drugs were sold from stalls on the main street, although political pressure and police clampdowns have stopped this open sale. Around 1,000 people live and work in this community, with its eclectic collection of restaurants, oddball architecture and a great concert venue, Loppen. However, as the Free Town stands on a piece of prime real estate in a fast-growing city, its existence is increasingly perceived as under threat – visit while you can. To get the most out of Christiania, take a guided tour (www.rundvisergruppen.dk; charge), run by local residents, departing from the main gate.

Opera House

From Christiania, continue along Prinsessegade to Holmen, where Copenhagen's modernist **Opera House** 28, which opened in 2005, dominates the former docklands site on the harbour front. Designed by Danish architect Henning Larsen, the building is topped by a

NOTES

Whether or not you're able to see an opera or ballet production at the city's new Opera House, a guided tour round the building is recommended – see the website https://kglteater.dk to book an appointment.

spectacular 'floating' roof. An elegant, pre-show restaurant is housed in the enormous, airy foyer. A number of the Nordic region's most eminent artists have contributed to the interior decor, including Per Kirkeby, responsible for the stunning bronze reliefs.

Outlying Districts

Highlights

- **Frederiksberg**, see page 74
- **Nørrebro**, see page 75
- **Bispebjerg**, see page 77

Although most of the main tourist attractions are clustered in and around the pretty old town, there are some gems worth seeking out in other areas of the city.

Frederiksberg

The leafy suburb of Frederiksberg (technically not part of Copenhagen, although it is surrounded by the city) is a great place for families. In summer, you can hire boats and row around the meandering canal system in rolling, romantic **Frederiksberg Have** (Frederiksberg Gardens; free). Look out for the colony of tame grey herons that wander the lawns and paths near the Chinese Pavilion. The gardens' southern end is dominated by the Baroque-style **Frederiksbarg Slot**, home to the Royal Danish Military Academy.

From the park, there's a good view of architect Norman Foster's famous elephant house at the **Zoologisk Have** (Copenhagen

Zoo; Roskildevej 32; www.zoo.dk; charge), home to tigers, brown bears, polar bears and a pride of lions. If you're in the area, it's worth paying a visit to the nearby **Glass Museum** (Cisternerne – Museet for Moderne Glaskunst; www.frederiksbergmuseerne.dk; charge), housed in an underground water tank: glowing glass, drips of water, and crypt-like arches lend it an almost medieval atmosphere.

Nørrebro

Nørrebro is another working-class district beginning the shift towards gentrification. **Skt Hans Torv** ㉙ and the surrounding streets contain some great cafés and restaurants, while interesting

Blue Planet National Aquarium Denmark

independent shops selling clothes and antiques are scattered along Elmegade and Ravnsborggade. It may sound odd, but one of the area's biggest attractions is **Assistens Cemetery** ㉚, where Copenhageners like to picnic, jog and play with their kids, alongside the graves of famous Danes like Hans Christian Andersen, Niels Bohr and Søren Kierkegaard.

Beyond Nørrebro, in Østerbro district, is Copenhagen's largest park, Fælledparken, At its eastern edge, just next to the Trianglen metro station, is **ENIGMA** (www.enigma.dk; charge). Relocated here in 2023, it's filled with fascinating, interactive displays on the history of communication, beginning with the establishment of the Danish postal service way back in 1624. A portion of the

Houses from the past at the Open-Air Folk Museum

museum is devoted to the rise of the internet and the current (and future) societal debates it has sparked. The name ENIGMA refers to the cipher machines once used for commercial and military communication, the oldest of which in the world is on display here, one of three to have survived to this day.

Bispebjerg

A 20-minute journey from Nørreport on the number 6A bus brings you to the immense **Grundtvigs Kirke** ㉛ (www.grundtvigskirke.dk; free) in the northwestern suburb of Bispebjerg. The church is a monument to N.F.S. Grundtvig (1783–1872), a renowned educationalist, austere parson and prolific hymn-writer. Built between 1921 and 1940, it is also a monument to early 20th-century Danish architecture. The church's design by Peder Jensen-Klint is simple but effective. Everything is in pale-yellow brick, from the 50m (160ft) tower to the altar.

Excursions

Highlights

- **Store Magleby and Dragør**, see page 78
- **Open-Air Folk Museum and Lyngby Lake**, see page 79
- **Arken**, see page 81
- **Louisiana Museum of Modern Art**, see page 81
- **Helsingør**, see page 82
- **Hillerød**, see page 84
- **Roskilde**, see page 86

In a country of 44,030 sq km (16,630 sq miles), nature has ingeniously divided Denmark into a land of more than 450 islands so that you are never more than 50km (30 miles) from the sea. Copenhageners have their own beach, woodlands and wide lake area, and it is easy to organise an excursion. Options include boat trips, windmill and water-mill sightings, a visit to a royal country castle, and the chance to explore two fabulous art galleries and a couple of pretty, traditional villages.

Store Magleby and Dragør

Travellers arriving by plane will already have visited Amager island – but there are far more charming places here than the international airport. A number 350S bus from Kongens Nytorv will take you south to the village of Store Magleby and then to charming Dragør. As many of the shops in Dragør are open on Sunday in summer, this is a good day to take the trip.

In an old farmhouse on the village street in **Store Magleby** you'll find **Amagermuseet** (Amager Museum; Hovedgaden 4 & 12; www.museumamager.dk; charge). The kitchen and bedrooms are furnished in the old style with items donated by local residents representing a strong Dutch connection in the area. Christian II (1513–23) invited a colony of Netherlands farmers to improve soil cultivation in the region, and to provide the royal table with 'as many roots and onions as are needed'. He gave the Dutch special privileges to live in Store Magleby, which for centuries was referred to as Hollænderbyen (Dutchmen's Town). They had their own judicial system and church, and developed a bizarre local costume.

The lovely 18th-century village of **Dragør** ㉜, 16km (10 miles) from the city, is remarkably well preserved. A walk among the half-timbered cottages with their postage-stamp-size gardens provides a vivid impression of what life was like two or more centuries ago. Beside the boat-filled harbour, a 1682 fisherman's cottage, the oldest house in the town, has been converted into **Dragør Museum** (Havnepladsen, Strandlinien 2 & 4; www.museumamager.dk; closed Mon and Oct–May; charge), devoted to local seafaring history.

Located just north of the airport, near the Kastrup metro station, the **Blue Planet National Aquarium Denmark** ㉝ (http://

denblaaplanet.dk; charge) will delight children and adults alike with its stunning spiralling architecture and, inside, sharks, moray eels and rays all swimming in impressive glass tanks. In the Amazon section you'll be able to walk through a hot and humid rainforest populated by birds, butterflies, piranhas and anacondas.

Grundtvigs Kirke, an early 20th-century masterpiece

Open-Air Folk Museum and Lyngby Lake

At Kongevejen 100, Kongens Lyngby, 16km (10 miles) north of the city, is **Frilandsmuseet** (www.natmus.dk; charge), the intriguing Open-Air Folk Museum. The museum is accessible by car along the A3 and A5 main roads, by bus number 184 from Nørreport terminus in town, or by regular S-train (line E) from Copenhagen Central Station to Sorgenfri station (a 25min ride).

Over 50 farmhouses, cottages, workshops and a Dutch-type windmill are scattered about the 35-hectare (90-acre) site – all furnished in the original style, even down to combs and portraits. Broadly, the buildings are split into geographical groups laid out along country lanes, together with bridges and village pumps, and all are authentically landscaped. Each building has been transplanted, tile by tile, timber by timber, from its original location. You'll find a Zealand group, a Jutland and a Faroes group, etc.

Homes of all classes are represented, from peasant to landowner, as well as artisan and farmer.

The smell of old timber and tar pervades the rooms. Geese and sheep are driven along the lanes. Displays of folk dancing, sheep shearing, threshing and weaving are given during the summer. There are horse-and-carriage rides and picnic spots in tree-lined meadows.

Allow yourself time to walk a kilometre towards **Lyngby** ㉞, where you can take a rural boat ride scarcely equalled in any capital city. On your left is the white-walled baroque castle, Sorgenfri Slot (closed to the public, although part of the gardens is accessible), built in the 18th-century by Lauridz de Thurah, who also designed the spire of Vor Frelsers Kirke (see page 71).

Pop Art at Louisiana

Proceed over Mølleåen (the Mill Stream). Follow the signs to the right for **Lyngby Sø - Bådfarten** (Lyngby Lake Boat Trip; Sorgenfrivej 23; baadfarten.dk; charge) to find two venerable canopied boats at the quayside. These have plied the four lakes since the 1890s. A 45-minute cruise, either Lyngby–Frederiksdal or Lyngby–Bagsværdvej, gives you the chance to savour the tree-covered backwaters and reedy lakes. Through the trees you'll also glimpse the 1803 mansion of Marienborg, the official summer residence of Danish prime ministers. Further on is Frederiksdal, with its castle on a hill above. This former royal house has been lived in by the same family since 1740. An alternative trip will take you to Sophienholm Mansion (1805), now a community cultural arts centre. Outdoor café tables give an idyllic view over the waters of Bagsværd Sø.

Back on Lyngby quay, it's a short walk to Lyngby S-train station for the return trip to the city.

Arken

Søren Robert Lund was just 25 years old and a student when he won a competition to design **Arken** ㉟ (www.arken.dk; charge), to house a museum of modern art on the waterfront about 20km (10 miles) west of Copenhagen. The building gives the impression of a ship nestling in the dunes, housing an ample permanent collection of contemporary art; Damien Hirst is well represented, as he donated eight pieces to the gallery in 2011. To reach it, take the S-train to Ishøj (lines A or E) then walk or take bus number 128 to the museum. To make a full day of it, bring your swimsuit – **Ishøj Strand**, one of the metropolitan area's best sandy beaches, is close by.

Louisiana Museum of Modern Art

If you have time for only one modern art museum, make it **Louisiana** ㊱ (Gammel Strandvej 13, Humlebæk; www.louisiana.dk; charge), a 30-minute train ride from Copenhagen. The museum is a work of art in itself: the main mid-19th-century mansion is extended by whitewashed galleries built into a hilly sculpture garden, with numerous glass walls blurring the boundaries between art and nature. The extensive collection includes works by Picasso, Warhol and Rauschenberg, COBRA artists such as Asger Jorn and, more recently, Per Kirkeby. A glazed corridor leads past a group of Giacometti figures to the excellent Museum Café. Its terrace – with stunning sea views – features metal mobiles by Alexander Calder.

In the gardens, you can picnic on the lawns while marvelling at Henry Moore's colossal bronze women silhouetted against the waters of the Øresund. There is an excellent range of daily children's activities, too. From Copenhagen's Central Station, take the regional train (Regionaltog) to Humlebæk station, from where it's a well-signposted 1km (0.6-mile) walk.

Helsingør

Further north along the coast, at the narrowest stretch of the Øresund, is Helsingør. On leaving the railway station, the town's most famous landmark comes into view – the UNESCO World Heritage site of **Kronborg Slot** ㊲ (Kronborg Castle; www.kronborg.dk; charge). To reach it on foot from the station takes about 20 minutes.

Many people will be familiar with Kronborg as 'Hamlet's castle of Elsinore'. No one knows if Shakespeare visited Kronborg personally, but some of his colleagues performed at the newly built castle, and so may have inspired him to set his tragedy here. Every summer the castle hosts performances of *Hamlet* in the courtyard.

The castle was built between 1574 and 1585 at the command of Frederik II for the purpose of extracting tolls from ships entering the narrow strait, and thus the Baltic (not a new idea – an earlier fortress on the site had also been a good money-spinner for the Danish treasury). Frederik, however, had more than just a stronghold in mind. He built a splendid Renaissance castle that could be lived in, peppered with ramparts, bastions, large windows and decorated towers. He sent for the Flemish architect Antonius van Opbergen to design the four-wing structure, then engaged various Danish and Dutch artists to paint, weave and indulge in decorative sculpture on a scale never before seen in Scandinavia.

The moated brick castle today stands as Frederik's proudest memorial, now sparsely furnished but immensely impressive. It has a feeling of solid strength and royal presence throughout, permeating the elaborate little chapel, the long galleries and stone stairways, and most of all the massive oak-beamed Great Hall – the largest of its kind in northern Europe. Now adorned with 12 paintings of the Øresund by Isaac Isaacsz, its walls were once hung with 40 tapestries by the Dutchman Hans Knieper, depicting the 113 Danish kings said to have reigned before Frederik II. Fourteen of the tapestries survive, and seven can be seen in a small room beneath the hall. Underneath the castle are extensive cellars and dungeons: you can take a tour of the cramped and creepy casemates, where the castle's besieged soldiers would have crouched in the darkness. This is also where you'll find Kronborg's most renowned exhibit, the statue of the nation's own mythical hero, Holger the Dane.

Helsingør has more to offer than the castle alone: there are medieval streets of colour-washed houses, the 15th-century **Skt Mariæ Kirke** and a **Carmelite Kloster** (Convent) to see, and the shiny **M/S Maritime Museum of Denmark** (www.mfs.dk; charge), opened in 2013 with interactive exhibitions honouring Denmark's seafaring prowesses past and present. A clever architectural trick, the uneven floors and irregular angles are evocative of sailing on a vessel.

Kronborg, Frederik II's Renaissance castle

Visits to Helsingør and to the Louisiana Museum of Modern Art may be readily combined. From Helsingør, board the train for Copenhagen, alighting at Humlebæk. Alternatively, at the bus terminal next to the railway station in Helsingør board a number 388 bus for the pleasant 25-minute journey along the coast to the museum. To return to Copenhagen from Louisiana turn left onto the main road to walk back to Humlebæk railway station.

Hillerød

Hillerød is the site of one of the greatest Renaissance castles in northern Europe, **Frederiksborg Slot** ❸❽ (Frederiksborg Castle; www.dnm.dk; charge), sometimes called the Nordic Versailles. This dazzling brick and sandstone castle is dramatically situated across three islands on a lake, and the best way to reach it is by way of a small boat that departs from the city centre. Although the oldest parts of the castle date from around 1560 and were built by Frederik II, most of the castle dates from between 1600 and 1620 – the work of that visionary Builder King, Christian IV. The style is Dutch Renaissance, and the result is spectacular. Danish monarchs resided here for about a century, and the absolute monarchs

Mythical hero: Holger the Dane at Kronborg Slot

were crowned in the palace chapel from 1671.

In 1859 much of the interior was destroyed by fire, but between 1860 and 1884 it was rebuilt with financial support from the brewer J.C. Jacobsen and later the Carlsberg Foundation. Since 1878 the castle has been the home of the **Danmarks Nationalhistoriske Museum** (National History Museum). This occupies more than 60 rooms and contains a complete record of the Danish monarchy, beginning with Christian I, who established the Oldenburg line (1448–1863), through all the monarchs of the following Glücksburg line to the present queen, Margrethe II. The exhibits are mostly in the form of portraits and paintings, with some pieces of period of furniture. But the rooms of the castle itself are perhaps of more interest to visitors. Riddersalen (the Knights' Hall) and the chapel are Frederiksborg's ultimate triumph. The 55m (185ft) Knights' Hall is awesome in its dimensions, with richly decorated tapestried walls, marble floor and carved wooden ceiling, all reconstructed from old drawings after the 1859 fire.

> **NOTES**
>
> Legend has it that this 9th-century Viking warrior never actually died, but just went to sleep, and will wake to defend Denmark if the country is threatened. During World War II, a section of the Resistance adopted the name of Holger Danske.

Below the Knights' Hall, Slotskirken (the chapel) escaped the fire, leaving its stunning gilt pillars and high vaulted nave virtually untouched. Almost every inch here is richly carved and ornamented. The chapel has inset black marble panels with quotations from the scriptures, marquetry panels in ebony and rare woods, and both its altar and pulpit in ebony with biblical scenes in silver relief. The organ is one of Europe's most notable, an almost unchanged original from 1610 by the Flemish master Esaias Compenius.

Around the gallery of this chapel hang the coats of arms belonging to knights of both the orders of the Elephant and the Grand

NOTES

Rungstedlund, midway along the coast between the city and Helsingør, was home to *Out of Africa* author Karen Blixen. The house is now a museum devoted to her eventful life (https://blixen.dk).

Cross of Danneborg. Some modern recipients are also represented, such as Sir Winston Churchill and General Eisenhower.

Hillerød is just 9km (5 miles) from Helsingør and it is possible to visit both places in the same day (although it would make for a hurried day trip). The two towns are 30 minutes apart using the half-hourly local train (Lokalbane) service. You can travel to Hillerød from Copenhagen by S-train (a 1hr journey on the A line). It's a 20min walk from the station or a 10min trip with bus numbers 301, 302 and 303.

Roskilde

According to legend, the Viking king Roar founded the town of **Roskilde** ㊴ around AD 600. Situated 30km (19 miles) to the west of Copenhagen, this neat little town has plenty to offer those who undertake the 25-minute train journey from the capital.

Once you arrive, head straight for the centre, towards the three green spires which dominate the flat landscape. This is Roskilde's splendid **Domkirke** (Cathedral; www.roskildedomkirke.dk; opening times can change at short notice, so check website; church: free; museum, royals chapels and tombs: charge), a UNESCO World Heritage site. One of the most remarkable buildings in Denmark, it began life as a wooden church built by King Harald Bluetooth around AD 1000, when he first converted to Christianity. In the 1170s, Bishop Absalon, founder of Copenhagen, built a brick-and-stone cathedral here for his new bishopric, and during the course of the next 300 years this grew into the Romanesque-Gothic amalgam of today.

Christian IV added the distinctive spires in 1635. He also erected his own burial chapel and a gilded royal pew in the north wall of the church, heavily latticed and shielded from public view so that (it is said) he could smoke his pipe in peace during Sunday services. Nearly all the Danish kings and queens since Margrete I (who died in 1412) are buried in sarcophagi and chapels all different from one another in a jumbled symphony of style.

On the south side, the chapel of King Frederik V is a simple design in white paint and Norwegian marble, with 12 tombs grouped around it. In contrast, the Christian IV chapel on the north side is marked by elaborately wrought ironwork from 1618 and interior decoration mainly from the 19th century featuring

Frederiksborg Slot, home to Danish monarchs for 200 years

frescoes, paintings depicting scenes from his reign, and bronze statues. In 2010, the medieval St Birgitte's Chapel received a very modern glass sarcophagus, designed by Bjørn Nørgaard, which will eventually hold the present queen Margrethe.

A light note is introduced by the clock high on the southwest wall of the nave: as each hour arrives, St George and his horse rear up, beneath them a dragon utters a shrill cry, a woman figure strikes her little bell four times with a hammer and a man rings his big bell once. The chapel on the outside of the cathedral beside the northwestern tower was inaugurated in 1985 and dedicated to the memory of Frederik IX, the King of Denmark from 1947–72, who is buried here.

To the front of the church is Stændertorvet, the traditional square of this old market town, lined with outdoor café tables in good weather, and fruit and vegetable stalls every Wednesday and Saturday morning. On Saturday there is also a popular flea market.

To the rear is parkland, where you can walk downhill through the meadow, towards the fjord and the **Vikingeskibsmuseet** (Viking Ship Museum; www.vikingeskibsmuseet.dk; charge). When 11th-century Danes wanted to block off the sea route to Roskilde from the marauding Norwegians, they sank five Viking ships across a narrow neck of the shallow fjord here. These ships,

ACROSS THE ØRESUND TO MALMÖ

The 8km (5-mile) long Øresund Bridge linking Denmark and Sweden, opened in 2000, renders a day-trip to Malmö another appealing option for those looking for an excursion. Sweden's third-largest city, Malmø (www.visitmalmo.se) has an attractive old town surrounding Stortorget, the main square. Trains take just 35 minutes, leaving Copenhagen Central Station every 15 minutes during the daytime, and roughly hourly between 11pm and 5am.

salvaged in 1962, now form the basis of the museum and are superbly displayed. They include a sturdy ocean-going trader and an awe-inspiring longship, the dreaded man o'war, used for long-range raiding. There's also a great café on sight with views of Roskilde Fjord

The museum building stands on the edge of the water with one side made completely of glass, bringing the fjord almost into its main room. The outline of each ship was first reconstructed in metal strips, then the thousands of pieces of wood were treated and placed in position. The museum is lavishly illustrated with photographs and charts, and free film shows (in English) recount the full story of the salvage.

Roskilde Cathedral, a UNESCO World Heritage Site

In recent years the Vikingeskibsmuseet has been developed into a fascinating complex in which you can see wooden boats being built by hand using the original skills, sail on one of these vessels, and eat in the attractive restaurant. Then, to end the day in a truly Viking flavour, you can sample a draught of the favourite brew of these hardy sailors, *mjød* (mead).

At the highest point on the museum's grounds, a brand-new construction was launched in 2024. Slated for completion in 2030, a grand wooden pavilion will become the new home for the museum's five famous ships.

GoBoat passes Papirøen (Paper Island)

Things to do

Most of Copenhagen's major attractions are set within walkable distance of the city's old centre, allowing you to experience its charms on an easy stroll down Strøget. Pop into its churches and museums, take in the views from its spires or from the top of the Round Tower, relax in its squares with a *pølse (Norwegian hot dog)* or pastry and glide beneath its bridges on a canal boat tour. Thanks to an excellent metro and bus system, even attractions beyond the core are easily reached. Alternatively, do as the Danes and traverse the city streets by bike – so long as you're committed to keeping the rules of the road. In the evenings, the world is your oyster here, with superlative dining and nightlife scenes; choose from brown pubs (low-key, dim-lit local bodegas) and jazz clubs to ritzy cocktail bars.

Culture

Art and design. Copenhagen has a thriving visual arts scene with a lengthy list of excellent galleries. For contemporary arts, head the streets around Nyhavn, home to renowned Nikolaj Kunsthal (Nikolaj Plads 10; www.nikolajkunsthal.dk), **Kunsthal Charlottenborg** (www.kunsthalcharlottenborg.dk) and the **Martin Asbæk Gallery** (Bredgade 23; martinasbaek.com). For a dose of iconic Danish design, head to the Designmuseum Danmark (Bredgade 68; www.designmuseum.dk), filled with elegant yet functional furniture – a true passion among Danes.

There's plenty more modern art on display in Kødbyen, the Meatpacking District, perhaps most notably at V1 (Slagtehusgade 44D; www.v1gallery.com), as well as on Refshaleøen, home to Copenhagen Contemporary (Refshalevej 173A; www.copenhagen contemporary.org).

Classical music, opera, ballet. Scores of concerts are held throughout the year at the branches of the Royal Theatre (www.kglteater.dk), the Royal Danish Academy of Music (www.dkdm.dk), Tivoli Gardens

A hand-painted piece by Royal Copenhagen Porcelain

and in various churches and museums. The Royal Theatre's splendid Opera House on Holmen hosts performances of opera and ballet, for which a small number of tickets is held back for sale on the day. The Royal Danish Ballet is internationally acclaimed, and rightly so – it is one of Europe's oldest, with a repertory going back 200 years. Nowadays, the company experiments in modern dance as well, but its great tradition lies in Bournonville classics, such as *La Sylphide* and *The Dancing School*. The company performs from September to June.

Jazz, folk, rock. Copenhagen is one of Europe's leading jazz centres. Jazzhus Montmartre (Regnegade 19A; www.jazzhusmontmartre.dk) is one of the city's premiere venues, hosting international, national and local artists. Mojo Blues Bar (Løngangsstræde 21C; www.mojo.dk) is another great live music venue that is usually packed to the brim. There's an annual 10-day Jazz Festival (www.jazz.dk), which is held at the beginning of July, plus a two-week-long Vinterjazz festival in February. There are several venues for folk music near the university. The main venues for local and international rock and pop concerts include Amager Bio (Øresundsvej 6; www.amagerbio.dk), Vega (www.vega.dk), Forum (www.forumcph.dk) and Royal Arena (www.royalarena.dk). Big names also play at Tivoli Gardens (www.tivoli.dk), while Loppen in Christiania (www.loppen.dk) attracts a more artistic clientele, there to see great local experimental, alternative, hardcore, world, jazz and rock shows. On summer Sundays free rock concerts are held in Fælled Parken.

Nightlife

Copenhagen is a great place for partying. Some of Copenhagen's cosy cafés become bars at night, and many of the city's best nightspots blur the line between bar and restaurant: often when the kitchen closes, a place will slide smoothly into 'club' mode, staying open late into the night. Alcohol is expensive, so there's a tendency for people to drink at home first and start hitting the town from 11pm onwards. 'In' places come and go, but trendy Vesterbro is the most plausible area to start: for a taste of the good life, try WarPigs (Flæsketorvet 25–37; www.warpigs.dk), a place famous for its craft Mikkeller's beers and excellent BBQ dishes. Nearby Jolene (Flæsketorvet 81–85; www.facebook.com/JoleneBar) is a quirky riot. Longstanding Vega (Enghavevej 40; www.vega.dk), a huge complex containing no fewer than 12 bars, is one of the city's biggest and best mainstream clubs. Locally brewed beers are popular – sample them at BrewPub (Vestergade 29; www.brewpub.dk), near the Rådhus; or at the award-winning microbrewery Nørrebro Bryghus (Ryesgade 3; www.noerrebrobryghus.dk). Also, in Nørrebro is the intimate, laid-back nightclub Rust (Guldbergsgade 8; www.rust.dk), with a minimalist, sci-fi atmosphere, which hosts top DJs and has great live shows.

Shopping

Where to shop

Shopping in Copenhagen is a quality experience, and the city's pedestrian precincts and attractive squares add to the pleasure of seeking out those special purchases. Undoubtedly the place to begin is Strøget (pronounced stroy-et), a charming pedestrian-only combination of four streets starting at Rådhuspladsen with Frederiksberggade, which leads into Nygade Vimmelskaftet, Amagertorv, Østergade, and ends in Kongens Nytorv. Along Strøget, said to be the longest pedestrian-only street in the world, you will find everything from antiques to avant-garde furniture, while established department stores such as Illum and Magasin du Nord offer the very best in Danish design. The finest ceramics, silver and crystal shops, superb home furnishings and interiors stores, the city's leading furriers, antiques shops, department stores, clothing shops and souvenir outlets exist harmoniously, side-by-side with a varied selection of restaurants and bars.

In the smaller streets branching off (and parallel to) Strøget is an eclectic array of music stores, potters and silversmiths, antiques shops and fashion boutiques. On the opposite side of Kongens Nytorv, and convenient for those visiting Amalienborg and the Marble Church, are Bredgade and Store Kongensgade. For up-and-coming designers, try bohemian Vesterbro.

VAT, or sales tax (in Danish MOMS), is 25 percent on all products and services. Foreign visitors (non-EU residents) who spend over 300kr in any one store displaying 'Tax-Free Shopping' stickers will be given a form to reclaim the tax when they leave the country. Ask for details in the shop, or check out the websites www.planetpayment.com or www.globalblue.com.

What to buy

Interior design, home accessories and furniture are the pride of Denmark, beloved by all Danes. For the best in show, head to Illums Bolighus (www.illumsbolighus.dk) or **Royal** Copenhagen (www.royalcopenhagen.com), each with stores in the heart of Strøget. The latter is an excellent place to exhaust your budget on world-famous, hand-painted porcelain. In business here since 1911, Royal Copenhagen's wares are all one of a kind, with no two pieces alike. **Danish furniture**, which ranks among the world's best, will

Shopping for antiques at City Hall Square (Rådhuspladsen)

often come with a black circular 'Danish Furniture-Makers' sticker attached. Items are credited to the designer rather than to the factory. Lamps are also lovingly designed, as are household textiles and hand-woven rugs. Many of the best stores for sofas, chairs and tables, and the things to put on them, are clustered around Strøget: Illums Bolighus (Amagertorv 10; www.illumsbolighus.dk); CasaShop (Store Regnegade 2; www.casashop.dk); Hay House (Østergade 61; www.hay.dk); Designer Zoo (Vesterbrogade 137; www.designerzoo.dk). Another favourite is up Vesterbrogade to the west: Paustian (Niels Hemmingsens Gade 24; www.paustian.dk).

Amber jewellery is also available, particularly in stores along Strøget. The local 'gem' (actually a fossil resin) may be cheaper here than at home, but beware, the quality can vary tremendously. Visit the House of Amber (www.houseofamber.com) on the approach to Nyhavn at Kongens Nytorv 2.

Hand-painted toy soldiers

Antiques are in plentiful supply, especially the second-hand/vintage rather than the fine-art variety. The locals flock to Bredgade, off Kongens Nytorv, and Ravnsborggade, in the Nørrebro neighbourhood, which contains a dozen of antiques shops and hosts the occasional flea market.

Aquavit *(akvavit)*, the local spirit, usually flavoured with caraway seed, is cheaper than imported spirits.

Knitwear comes Nordic-style, often highly patterned, warm, and, in some cases, expensive. There are knitwear shops all over the city; some sell wool and patterns for those who are tempted to set about knitting their own garments.

Stereo equipment. The very latest in sound systems, TVs and speakers can be found at the Bang & Olufsen Centre (http://stores.bang-olufsen.com), at Østergade 18.

Silver is another Danish speciality, dominated by the name Georg Jensen (www.georgjensen.com). Silver in Denmark is quality-controlled and should always be hallmarked. The Jensen showrooms at Amagertorv 4 offer creations that range from key rings to highly precious jewellery.

Souvenirs are myriad. Little Mermaid figures, Copenhagen dolls in frilly skirts and black lace caps, blue ceramic figurines and animals, and countless trolls and Vikings abound, as well as hand-painted spoons, racks and pepper mills. A particularly attractive Danish keepsake is an Amager shelf – a group of three or four small hand-painted shelves in a triangular frame that hangs on the wall. Beware, however, of cheap versions.

Toys are simple and attractive, especially those in solid wood. You'll also see hundreds of the Danish wooden soldiers in all sizes. Of course, when it comes to toys that are fun and educational, the Danish invention Lego is the daddy of them all – their flagship store is on Strøget (Vimmelskaftet 37; www.lego.com).

Clocks and watches. Gullacksen Ure, Frederiksberggade 8 on Strøget, may not be the largest clock shop, but its owner is the third generation of an old watchmaking family. Besides a wide selection of Danish and international brand-name watches, clocks, barometers and hygrometers, look for the museum pieces on the walls. Of particular interest are the practical Jacob Jensen temperature stations.

Illums Bolighus

Outdoor activities

There are plenty of sporting activities to suit every taste within easy reach of the city. The top spectator sport is football (soccer), while popular participation sports include sailing and fishing. Ask the nearest Danish tourist office (see page 137) for an up-to-date list of what's available.

NOTES

Please check out site www.visitcopenhagen.com/copenhagen/shopping for an insider's guide to some of Copenhagen's best shopping quarters.

Boating. Steer yourself through Copenhagen's waterways on an electric GoBoat (goboat.dk), available even for those with zero boating experience (they aren't especially fast). Book online before showing up at the docks at Islands Brygge.

Cycling. Some hotels lend bicycles to their guests at no charge. Otherwise they're easy to hire (see page 127). You can use the extensive network of cycle paths *(cykelsti)* without any worry about cars, or indeed the weather – if it starts raining, country buses and trains will carry your bike and taxis have bicycle racks. To avoid local wrath, signal clearly: as a brake light, raise your forearm; point your arms as blinkers.

Fishing. Jutland is Denmark's sea-fishing capital, but you can still go for Øresund cod, mackerel, gar-pike, or flat-fish from Amager and the coast to the north of the city. A state angling licence must be purchased online (www.fisketegn.dk; 46/150/214kr per day/week/year) or at campsites, fishing-tackle shops and tourist offices. You can rent licensed boats on Lyngby, Furesø and Bagsværd lakes on the northwest edge of Copenhagen.

Football. The Danish football team competes at the highest level, and the sport has an enthusiastic following. The main Copenhagen stadium is at Parken (www.parkenstadion.dk), the home ground of F.C Copenhagen and the Danish national team.

Horse racing. The racetrack *(Galopbane)* at Klampenborg (www.galopbane.dk) is open mainly on Saturdays from mid-April–late October. To get there, take the regional train (Regionaltoget) RE2101 towards Helsingør, or the S-train, alighting at Klampenborg, then catch bus number 388 in the Lyngby direction.

Skating. Numerous stretches of water within the capital's boundaries freeze up in winter and outdoor rinks *(skøjtebaner)* are set up in the city centre, such as at Frederiksberg Runddel and Kongens Nytorv.

Skiing. Opened as a recreational centre in 2018 on the sloping roof of power station, CopenHill (www.copenhill.dk) puts its shape to good use. Rather than snow, the piste's surface is synthetic, allowing for us year-round. Book online and arrive at least 30min prior to your appointment to gear up. But there's no need to put on skis to ascend the hill – the trail and elevator are free during business hours, offering a glimpse into the cutting-edge factory and wonderful city vistas from the top.

Swimming. There is good sea bathing along the Zealand coast

The grand interior of the Royal Theatre, built in 1874

north and south of Copenhagen, but the sea is rarely warm. Nude bathing is mainly at Tisvildeleje on the north coast. There are about a dozen indoor swimming pools in Copenhagen, some with sauna/massage and gym facilities, and several outdoor pools which are open from mid-May until the end of August. So successful has the clean-up of the Inner Harbour been that there is now a fantastically popular outdoor swimming pool (*havnebade*; literally 'harbour bath') at Islands Brygge (open year-round from 6am–10pm; lifeguard on duty June–Aug 10am–6pm), with diving towers and a green lawn full of picnickers in front. Another wonderful facility is Amager Strandpark, a vast man-made beach and lagoon just 5km (3 miles) from the city centre, where Copenhageners flock

Football is Denmark's most popular spectator sport

to swim, run, skate, and play beach volleyball. There are Metro stations at three places along the beach: Øresund, Amager Strand and Femøren.

Watersports. Rent a kayak to glide through the canals of the city on your own from Kayak Bar (Børskaj 12; www.kayakrepublic.dk). On offer here are both beginner-friendly, sit-on-top kayaks and, for experienced kayakers only, sea kayaks. Alternatively, at the same location, give back through the Green Kayak (www.greenkayak.org) initiative, whereby rental is free so long as you pledge to collect floating trash along the way. At Amager Strandpark (see above), you can also rent kayaks from Kajakhotellet (www.kajakhotellet.dk) or learn to kite-surf with Amager Kiteskole (www.amagerkiteskole.dk). Water-skiing is popular on the Furesø, and it is possible to windsurf in Vedbæk harbour – consult the tourist office for details.

NOTES

If you are fortunate enough to be invited to a Danish home, don't turn down the opportunity. The Danes love to entertain and set great store by creating a cosy yet chic atmosphere for guests.

Copenhagen for children

Amusement parks. Tivoli (see page 33) should certainly appeal to the entire family. Less well known than Tivoli – and generally considered to be a rather downmarket version – is Bakken (Apr–Aug; www.bakken.dk), which is very popular with Danes. Situated on the outskirts of Klampenborg, just a 12-minute train ride from the city centre, it has 33 rides, dozens of cafés and restaurants and the country's most famous revue show. Entry to the park is free, and an all-ride pass costs 329kr when bought at the gate (279kr in advance online).

Museums and attractions. The Experimentarium Science Centre (Tuborg Havnevej 7, Hellerup; www.experimentarium.dk) is a lively place where children are positively encouraged to tinker around with exhibits. The ENIGMA (Øster Allé 3; www.enigma.dk) museum has an entire section wholly devoted to kids, as do Nationalmuseet (see page 52), Statens Museum for Kunst (see page 59) and Louisiana (see page 81). The Danish War Museum (Tøjhusgade 3; www.natmus.dk) features a magnificent display of shining armour, model planes, giant cannons and ship models. The Viking Ship Museum (www.vikingeskibsmuseet.dk) at Roskilde (see page 88) offers tours on the water in replica Viking ships during summer months and other workshops aimed at children.

Offering horse-drawn carriage tours to the city's north, Frilandsmuseet (see page 79; www.natmus.dk) always goes down well with children too. At Christiansborg kids can visit the Royal Stables (see page 49) and see the coaches and the horses that pull them.

There are plenty of rides to enjoy at Tivoli Gardens

Copenhagen's Zoologisk Have (see page 74), established more than 120 years ago, is a good place to spend an afternoon. It houses more than 2,500 animals and has a fine children's section, restaurant and cafeteria. Den Blå Planet (The Blue Planet; Jacob Fortlingsvej 1, 2770 Kastrup; www.denblaaplanet.dk) opened in 2013 in an amazing swirl-shaped building on Amager Island (visible as you're coming in to land at the international airport and a 10min walk from Kastrup Metro station). The 50 aquariums (see page 78) contains over 23,000 animals, including piranha, sea lions and hammerhead sharks.

Swimming. Indoors, Vandkulturhuset at the DGI sports centre (Tietgensgade 65; www.dgibyen.dk) is a state-of the-art swimming complex with facilities for children of all ages. Outdoors, the Islands Brygge harbour swimming pool (see page 99) has two children's sections.

Tours. Canal trips are a must (see page 131). Worth considering are boat cruises, such as those from Lyngby (see page 80).

Festivals and events

Most of Copenhagen's annual festivals involve music. For an up-to-the-minute guide to what's on, visit the Copenhagen Visitor Centre (see page 137) or check out www.visitcopenhagen.com/search/whatson.

January Copenhagen's four-day, biannual Fashion Week (www.copenhagenfashionweek.com) is the largest of its kind in Northern Europe, making waves across the city at the end of this month and in August.

February Vinterjazz: three weeks of winter jazz. Frost Festival: a month of pop/electronic gigs in unusual venues around the city.

Shrovetide Beating the Barrel, parades and carnival festivities, centred around Rådhuspladsen and the Nationalmuseet.

March CPH:DOX (www.cphdox.dk), one of the world's largest documentary film festivals, runs for roughly 10 days.

April Queen's birthday (16 April): crowds gather outside Amalienborg Slot at noon for the Queen's balcony appearance.

May Marches and brass bands converge on Fælledparken (the city's largest park) on May Day. Copenhagen Marathon held in May. Distortion (www.cphdistortion.dk): 100,000 ravers join a citywide party (late May/early June).

Open-air swimming at Islands Brygge

Whitsuntide Copenhagen Carnival: colourful Latin-style processions and hundreds of bands attract large numbers of spectators.

June St Hans Eve (23 June): bonfires burn to celebrate the longest day. Roskilde Festival (roskilde-festival; late June/early July): Denmark's biggest rock festival. There's also Distortion (www.cphdistortion.dk), with city-wide street parties featuring electronic music, and CopenHell (www.copenhell.dk), the country's largest metal event.

July Copenhagen Jazz Festival (www.jazz.dk): bands play every jazz style from bebop onwards, on stage, in pubs and on the streets.

August Copenhagen Historic Grand Prix (www.chgp.dk): vintage cars take to the streets. Copenhagen Pride: five-day LGBTQ+ event culminating in a colourful parade. Kulturhavn: harbour-based festival, with music, dancing and family fun.

September Golden Days Festival: celebrates a different era of Copenhagen's history each year with all manner of cultural events. Blues Festival: concerts at venues across the city.

October Night of Culture: museums, galleries, churches, libraries and theatres open their doors after dark. Mix Copenhagen: gay and lesbian film festival.

November–December Tivoli is transformed into a winter wonderland with glittering illuminations, ice-skating and a Christmas market.

Food and drink

Food is a national obsession in Denmark, most often served to a very high standard. As Scandinavia's culinary capital, its restaurants have boosted the global brand of Nordic cuisine, underlined by a celebration of seasonal, locally sourced ingredients. Copenhagen can comfortably count more Michelin stars than anywhere else in Scandinavia, but even at the city's more modest offerings you'll find quality ingredients and an impressive attention to detail. Thanks to a blossoming of variety in recent years, Copenhagen's restaurant roster includes plenty of Middle Eastern mezze, Vietnamese pho and Indian curries in addition to traditional staples like *smørrebrød* (open-faced sandwiches) and *fiskefrikadeller* (fish cakes). Indeed, the days when street food was limited to the traditional hotdog stands (still excellent) are long gone, with falafel, shawarma, wood-fired pizza and gourmet burgers always within easy reach.

NOMA

Launched in 2003, the restaurant *Noma* has caused more than a stir in the Danish food scene, aptly named for the cuisine it helped bring into the global spotlight: *nordisk mad* (Nordic food). In addition to its three Michelin stars, it's been named nine times among the world's top restaurants by *Restaurant* magazine, winning the number one spot in 2010, 2011, 2012, 2014 and 2021. Largely the fruit of foraging, their sensational tasting menu has always been wholly dependent on the season, with Nordic delicacies ranging from horse mussels and deep-sea crabs to truffles, musk ox and elderberries. In 2022, *Noma* hit headlines again by announcing that it would close its doors at the end of 2024, shifting its role from restaurant to "food lab" in pursuit of further innovation. In this new phase, Noma's many fans will need to watch for sporadic pop-ups and special events, to be announced on their website and held both here in Copenhagen and around the world.

Top 10 things to try

1. Flæskesteg

Quintessential Danish, *flæskesteg* – fried, grilled or oven-roasted pork belly – is the country's traditional Christmas dish. But far from reserved for the holidays, it features regularly on the daily menu of Copenhagen restaurants. In the 1860s, after the Industrial Revolution, wood-fired stoves were put into domestic use, which caused a revolution on Danish tables. Pork, loved by the Danes, has been served in a baked form since then. Traditionally, to make *flæskesteg*, pork loin from the breast or neck is baked without removing the skin, after the rind is then cut into narrow strips so that the baking process gives you the crispy crack-lings that are essential for this dish. The meat is sea-soned with salt, pepper, bay leaves and cloves.

Sleek Danish dining

2. Smørrebrød

Smørrebrød (open-faced sandwiches) are thickly but-tered slices of heavy Danish rye bread covered with one of a wide array of delicacies: liver pâté *(leverpostej)*, veal *(kalvekød)*, ham *(skinke)*, roast beef *(stegt oksekød)*, salmon *(laks)*, smoked eel *(røget ål)*, shrimp *(reje)*, cod roe *(torskerogn)*, pickled herring *(sild)*, a variety of salads *(salat)* or cheese *(ost)*.

It's often served with a rémoulade or thick spread of mayonnaise, and is garnished with various accessories that have been carefully chosen to enhance both taste and appearance. Larger restaurants have scores of different *smørrebrød*. Often, you'll be given a pencil to mark your menu with what kind you'd like and your desired type of bread (*rugbrød*: dark rye; *franskbrød:* white). Don't confuse your *smørrebrød* with the Swedish word *smorgasbord*. The famous Scandinavian buffet-style spread is known in Denmark as *det store kolde bord* (the cold table), and usually offers a bewildering array of dishes.

3. Koldskål

A deliciously sweet and tart buttermilk soup, *koldskål* (literally: 'cold bowl') is especially popular with the locals during the warmer summer months. More of a snack than a meal, it's typically made from *kærnemælk* (buttermilk), and sometimes also *tykmælk* (soured milk, not unlike yoghurt), lemon and vanilla. Although *koldskål* can be eaten plain, it is traditionally complemented with crunchy kammerjunkere cookies crumbled on top.

4. Pickled herring

Marinated herring has been a staple in Northern Europe since the Middle Ages when it was used as a means of storing and transporting fish. The herring was pickled and then barrel-packed for storage or transport. The traditional curing of herring takes place in two parts: firstly, it is cured with salt to extract the water, then the salt is removed before the herring is marinated in a solution of vinegar, salt and sugar, often with the addition of peppercorns, bay leaves and raw onion. This gives the fish its rich flavour and aroma. In Copenhagen's restaurants, herring is usually found on the menu among the starters, accompanied by onions, capers, sometimes a yellow curry salad or a boiled egg – and always with traditional, dark rye bread.

5. Ristet Hotdog

The Danish hotdog is a core cultural experience not to be missed in Copenhagen, where hotdog stands (*pølsevogne*) are ubiquitous. Either roasted or boiled, the *pølse* (sausage) is either vividly red or brown. The classic *ristet med det hele* ('roasted with everything') comes with pickles, raw and fried onions, mustard, ketchup and remoulade in a sweet roll. As opposed to the traditional open hotdog bun, the *fransk hotdog* is ingeniously inserted into a hollow, tube-shaped bun, allowing for easy consumption on-the-go. In either case, wash your hotdog down with a Cocio, the Danes' beloved chocolate milk drink. Next to Rundetårn, you'll find DØP (Den Økologiske Pølsemand), a typically unassuming stand with all organic sausages (vegan and gluten-free alternatives available).

Street-side drinking

6. Frikadeller

Move over, Sweden: Denmark's got tasty meatballs too! Eaten here for at least 200 years, *frikadeller* are Danish meatballs that are usually made with ground pork, with the occasional addition of ground veal, and a little filler like flour, oats or breadcrumbs before being pan-fried in butter until browned. About as commonly encountered are *fiskefrikadeller* (fish cakes), in which the pork is replaced with cod and sometimes a little portion of salmon added. A staple on restaurant menus in the city, these delicious snacks are typically served with boiled potatoes with some traditional Danish brown sauce on the side, although pickled vegetables, mustard and rye bread are often served as an accompaniment.

Wienerbrød ('Vienna bread')

7. Coffee

Coffee *(kaffe)* – rich, strong and served with milk – can be found anywhere in Denmark, where Danes consistently rank among the world's most serious coffee drinkers. Copenhagen in particular is known for serving excellent coffee, courtesy of a talented and tight-knit community of coffee folk. Pick up a coffee on the run from any number of coffee stalls in the capital. If you fancy sipping your coffee in peace, head to Democratic in Copenhagen's public library. It's one long room with floor-to-ceiling windows and an assortment of coffee-table books, newspapers and notes scattered along the length of the bar table. For high-end speciailty coffee, head to Prolog in Kødbyen, where they roast their own beans – and definitely don't ask for syrup.

8. Danish Pastries

You'd do well to start your mornings in Copenhagen at a good *konditori* or *bageri* (patisserie or bakery) to sample the various types of pastry. Often designated outside Denmark as 'Danish pastry', *wienerbrød* ('Vienna bread') – the umbrella term for a range of flaky, sweet pastries – was first introduced in Denmark by Austrian bakers but has since become an essentially Danish speciality. The yeast dough is made from wheat flour, milk, eggs, sugar and lashings of butter or margarine before being carefully spread with butter and folded repeatedly to form 27 layers. It is a time-consuming and laborious process, but the rewards are delicious. Recent years have seen a blossoming of trendy bakeries around Copenhagen, among them the award-winning Juno the Bakery. The best draw long lines of locals happy to pay a premium on their pastry-fix. The most popular and ubiquitous varieties of wienerbrød you'll find are *kanelsnegl* (cinnamon roll)

Herring – New Nordic-style

TIPPING

Danes are not tip-minded, although good practice is to round up your bill after your meal. At very good restaurants, after excellent service, showing your appreciation with up to a 5 percent tip is always appreciated.

and *spandauer* (sweet bun with a custard filling; what many non-Danes would refer to as a 'Danish').

9. Beer

Danes have always loved their beer, with Danish mega-brewers Tuborg and Carlsberg the longstanding heavyweights here. Microbreweries, however, continue to gain ground with a raft of small-scale labels on the rise. Leading the charge are Mikkeller and To Øl, both pioneers in the scene, one characterized by an emphasis on quality, creativity and, often, quirk. You'll find plenty of beer bars featuring craft brews in Vesterbro and Nørrebro in particular, most offering everything from IPAs and stouts to wheat beers, pilsners and lagers.

10. Schnaps and wine

Akvavit is fiery Danish schnapps (in Danish, *snaps*) made from potatoes, often with a caraway taste. The colour varies according to the herbs and spices that have been used for flavouring. It is sipped at mealtimes during the opening fish course or with the cheese, and will sometimes be washed down with a beer chaser. If you order *akvavit* with your meal, the bottle may occasionally be put on the table for you to help yourself. Don't be deluded into thinking you'll only be charged for a single measure – back at the bar they'll know exactly how much has gone.

All wines are imported from France, Germany or Italy, and they are always expensive in restaurants. Even cheap house wine *(husets*

SKÅL! ...AND TAK!

Learn to say *skål* (the vowel is between 'loll' and 'hall') with your beer or *akvavit*. It's more than just Danish for 'cheers', it's a ritual if you are invited to a Danish home. Your host usually has the privilege of making the first toast, and will raise a glass, point it towards everyone in turn, looking directly at them, and say *'skål!'*. After all have taken a sip or a swallow, the host will look at each again in turn before putting down the glass.

After the meal itself, the appropriate – and essential – words to say are *'tak for mad'* (roughly pronounced *'tak for mel'*), meaning, very simply, 'thanks for the meal'.

vin) may be three times the supermarket price. After your dinner, try the Danish cherry liqueur, *Cherry Heering*.

Where to eat

There are more than 2,000 restaurants, cafés, bars and snack bars in Copenhagen. Copenhagen has more than its fair share of fine dining restaurants, with a whopping 26 Michelin stars as of this writing. For a drink, drop into one of the numerous cafés, pubs or bars dotted throughout the city. You'll also find *frokostrestauranter*: cosy, lunch-only restaurants, often offering good value and old-world charm, and are frequented by Danes themselves. If you're feeling indecisive, avoid the popular and central food market of Torvehallerne, where no less than 80 restaurants and delis share a single space.

When to eat

For Danes, breakfast *(morgenmad)* is a full meal rather than a snack. Likewise, breakfast in a Danish hotel is a far cry from the Spartan 'continental breakfast' of a roll and a cup of coffee. Bread rolls, cold cuts, cheeses, jam, pastries and probably eggs are all accompanied by milk and fruit juice followed by tea or coffee. Danes usually prefer a cold lunch, often *rugbrød* (ryebread) with some kind of cold cut – a sort of everyday version of *smørrebrød*. For genuine *smørrebrød*, head to a *frokostrestaurant*, which are only open during lunch hours. Dinner is served relatively early (around 6pm), and most restaurants stop serving at 9 or 10pm and are closed on Sunday and Monday.

Seafood favourites

In Denmark, fish (or small canapés) is the traditional first course of a full meal. It is also available as a main course, and a great variety of fish appears on the Danish menu. Herring is one of the firm favourites, and may be served pickled or fried, with a

Torvehallerne

sherry, vinegar, curry or fennel dressing. Succulent red Greenland shrimps are also popular. Lobster is also offered – though it is not cheap – as is crab, cod and halibut. Plaice features frequently in the local cuisine and may be served boiled or fried with a garnish of shellfish or parsley.

One great Scandinavian delicacy is *gravad laks*, in which raw salmon is pressed with salt and a small amount of sugar, and then sprinkled generously with chopped dill. A creamy sauce of oil, mustard and sugar is traditionally served alongside as an accompaniment. A summer seafood speciality is *danske rejer*, small pink shrimps from local waters that are served piled high on white bread.

Creamy desserts

To Help You Order ...

Could we have a table? **Kan vi få et bord?**

Do you have a set menu? **Har I en fast menu?**

I'd like a/an/some ... **Jeg vil gerne have ...**

beer **en øl**
bread **brød**
coffee **kaffe**
dessert **en dessert**
fish **fisk**
glass **et glas**
ice cream **is**
meat **kød**
menu **et spisekort**
milk **mælk**
mustard **sennep**
napkin **en serviet**
pepper **peber**
potatoes **kartofler**
salad **en salat**
salt **salt**
soup **suppe**
sugar **sukker**
tea **te**
vegetables **grønsager**
(iced) water **(is) vand**
wine **vin**

...and Read the Menu

agurkesalat cucumber salad
blomkål cauliflower
citron lemon
flæskesteg roast pork and crackling
grøn peber green pepper
grønne bønner French beans
gulerødder carrots
hamburgerryg loin of pork
hindbær raspberry
jordbær strawberry
kartoffelmos mashed potatoes
kirsebær cherry
kotelet chop
kylling chicken
kål cabbage
lagkage layer cake
lever liver
løg onion
mælk milk
medisterpølse pork sausage
nyre kidney
oksekød beef
pommes frites French fries
porre leek
rødkål red cabbage
ssvinekød pork
øtunge sole
æble apple
æg egg
æggekage omelette

Places to eat

The restaurant prices in this section are based on the cost of an average three-course evening meal (set menu) for one person, including tax but excluding drinks.
$$$$ = over 700kr
$$$ = 450–700kr
$$ = 300–450kr
$ = below 300kr

Around Rådhuspladsen and Vesterbro

Andersen Bakery Thorshavnsgade 26, Copenhagen S; www.andersen-bakery-eu.dk. This award-winning bakery traces its roots to the 1960s in Japan, where its first branches offered a taste of Copenhagen. Since arriving in Denmark in 2008, the bakery has made waves for its quality cakes and subtly Japanese touch. **$**

Bang & Jensen Istedgade 130, Copenhagen V; www.bangogjensen.dk. A chilled-out café-bar with a bohemian vibe, *Bang & Jensen* is perfect for everything from breakfast to a late-night beer. There's a small menu of light home-made meals, including sandwiches, chilli con carne, pasta and baba ganoush. **$**

Chicky Grill Bar Halmtorvet 21, Copenhagen V; tel: 33 22 66 96. No-nonsense and affordable Danish food served in a homey little brown-panelled bar with booth seating. Portions are substantial, and it's a wonderful place to try traditional *flæskesteg* (pork roast), served with potatos and gravy. For an authentic experience, wash it all down with a bottled Carlsberg. **$**

Formel B Vesterbrogade 182, Frederiksberg C; https://formelb.dk. This Michelin-starred restaurant offers an impeccable gastronomic experience. Classical French cooking is honed with Danish raw materials inspired by the modern European kitchen. **$$$$**

Hija de Sanchez Taqueria Slagterboderne 8, Copenhagen V; https://lovesanchez.com. Tiny spot in Kødbyen run by a former *Nova* pastry-chef, Rosio Sanchez, offering some of Copenhagen's very best Mexican cuisine: a small but excellent selection of tacos and sides like *esquites* (Mexican street corn). Order a margarita and soak up the Kødbyen coolness by tables out front when the weather allows. **$$**

Restaurant Klubben Enghavevej 4-6, Copenhagen V; www.restaurant-klubben.dk. A rough-and-ready Vesterbro pub, popular with locals, that serves generous portions of traditional home cooking: herring, fried bacon, *frikadeller* with creamed cabbage. Also has outdoor seating perfect for summer drinking. **$$**

Kodbyens Fiskebar Flæsketorvet 100, Copenhagen V; tel: 32 15 56 56; www.fiskebaren.dk. This popular place in the heart of the Meatpacking District shows off Scandinavia's fish and seafood to great effect – think sea urchins from Norway, Limfjorden oysters, char from Lake Vättern. If you don't have a restaurant reservation, you might get a seat at the bar. **$$**

Mother Høkerboderne 9-15, Copenhagen V; https://mother.dk. One of the best-value restaurants in trendy Kødbyen, serving scrumptious sourdough pizzas to hungry crowds. Also very popular are its weekends-only, Italian-style brunch (11am–3pm). Reservations are taken only up to 8pm, then it's a free-for-all. **$**

Nimb Berstorffsgade 5, Copenhagen V; https://nimb.dk. The wonderful Moorish Palace in Tivoli contains two smart bars, a pastry shop and three top-rated restaurants: the family-friendly brasserie, the Bar'n'Grill, and the Terrace, a French-inspired bistro. **$$$$**

Paté Paté Slagterboderne 1, Copenhagen V; www.patepate.dk. Fashionable yet friendly, this relaxed restaurant in the hip Kødbyen district serves up delicious French, Spanish and Moroccan food at big shared tables. With its candlelit bistro feel and huge wine list, it really comes into its own at night. **$$$**

Rio Bravo Vester Voldgade 86, Copenhagen V; https://riobravo.dk. A no-nonsense cowboy-style steakhouse, where even the seats at the bar are saddles. Still, the menu is heavy on Danish specialties too. If you've arrived with an appetite, order the *stegt flæsk* ad libitum: all-you can-eat fried pork belly with potatoes and a white parsley gravy. A popular place with Copenhagen's late-night revellers. **$$**

Tivoli Food Hall Bernstorffsgade 3, Copenhagen V; www.tivoli.dk. Accessible from both inside and out of the park, this food court features 15 food stalls with something for everyone, including sushi, burgers, sourdough pizzas, tacos and *smørrebrød*, making it a great stop for a meal in between rides. **$**

Les Trois Cochons Værnedamsvej 10, Copenhagen V; https://cofoco.dk. On the edge of Vesterbro and Frederiksberg, this place is worth the walk for the good-value food, attractive surroundings and its position on Copenhagen's self-confessed foodie street. Housed in an old butcher's shop, it serves up gourmet, hearty French bistro food amongst candles, chandeliers and glass-panelled cabinets. **$$**

Strøget and Beyond

Restaurant L'Alsace Ny Østergade 9/Pistolstræde, Copenhagen K; https://alsace.dk. Looking out onto a charming courtyard surrounded by 17th-century buildings, this restaurant has an interesting menu grounded in French and Austrian cuisines. Great-value too. Try the excellent shellfish soup, French omelette or ribeye au poivre. **$$**

Café Sorgenfri Brolæggerstræde 8, Copenhagen K; https://cafesorgenfri.dk. First opened in 1929, this charmingly antiquated *frokostrestaurant* (lunch only) boasts a central location and an excellent reputation for its classic Danish *smørrebrød*, roast pork and *frikadeller*. **$**

Conditori La Glace Skoubogade 3, Copenhagen K; https://laglace.dk. A must-visit for any sweet tooth, this patisserie opened its doors in 1870, remaining among the most venerated patisseries in a country that prides itself on cakes and pastries. Try the famous (and ironically named) "Sportskage", consisting of crushed nougat, whipped cream, a macaroon bottom and caramelized choux pastry – well worth the calories and the upmarket price. **$$**

Husmanns Vinstue Larsbjørnsstræde 2, Copenhagen K; https://husmannsvinstue.dk. Housed in an old cellar since 1888, this still-popular restaurant serves up an excellent Danish lunch in cosy surrounds. If struggling to order, consider asking for the invariably traditional *dagens ret* (dish of the day). **$$**

Kanal Caféen Frederiksholms Kanal 18, Copenhagen K; www.kanalcafeen.dk. Enjoy a *smørrebrød* in a maritime atmosphere at this excellent Danish lunch restaurant, in business since 1852. Step down from street level into a warren of cosy rooms, and feast on herring, meatballs and smoked salmon from Bornholm. **$**

Københavner Caféen Badstuestræde 10, Copenhagen K; https://kobenhavnercafeen.dk. Handily situated just off Strøget, heading south in the direction of Gammel Strand, this place is particularly recommended for its self-titled platter, combining no less than nine favourite types of *smørrebrød*. **$$**

Kong Hans Kælder Vingaardsstræde 6, Copenhagen K; https://konghans.dk. This lovely cellar restaurant, with its swooping Gothic arches and two

Michelin stars, is one of Denmark's finest. Since 1876 it has served classical French cuisine, always freshened with the best ingredients of the season. Reservations required. **$$$$**

Krogs Fiskerestaurant Gammel Strand 38, Copenhagen K; www.krogs.dk. Justly renowned for its excellent seafood dishes, this Danish institution is set on historic Gammel Strand, site of the city's old fish market, housed in an 18th-century building with classy, early-20th-century décor. Reservations highly recommended. **$$$**

Madklubben Store Kongensgade 66, Copenhagen K; www.madklubben.dk. A riposte to the highfalutin side of the Copenhagen dining scene, Madklubben is an unpretentious place that serves fabulous food, but keeps costs low by offering a short-and-simple menu with surcharges for more expensive dishes. This particular restaurant, near the Marble Church, is the first of what has become a Danish food empire. **$**

RizRaz Kanikkestræde 19, Copenhagen K; www.rizraz.dk. RizRaz does a splendid Mediterranean vegetarian buffet with plenty of vegan options (spinach lasagne, falafel, tabouleh, etc.) for 145kr at lunch, 185kr in the evening; for meat-eaters, there also burgers and steaks. **$**

Slotskælderen hos Gitte Kik Fortunstræde 4, Copenhagen K; https://slotskaelderen.dk. Come to this delightfully cosy basement *frokostrestaurant*, first opened in 1797, for *smørrebrød, beer and schnapps*, and perhaps to rub shoulders with Danish politicians (just across the canal is Christiansborg, home of the Danish Parliament). **$–$$**

Tight Hyskenstræde 10, DK-1207 Copenhagen K; www.tight-cph.dk. This classy and comfortable café-restaurant presents a small but carefully chosen selection of Nordic dishes, all with an international twist. They're all winners, from the Teriyaki-glazed venison carpaccio to the sweet potato veggie burger. **$$**

University Quarter and Parks

Restaurant AOC Dronningens Tværgade 2, Copenhagen K; https://restaurantaoc.dk. Boasting two Michelin stars, this elegant restaurant occupies a cellar in one of the city's old palaces, a few minutes' walk from Rosenborg Slot and the King's Garden. Diners are treated to a 17-course 'sensory menu', excelling in the gastronomic innovation typical of Copenhagen's top restaurants. **$$$$**

Café & Ølhalle 1892 Rømersgade 22, Copenhagen N; https://cafeogoelhalle.dk. Set within Arbejdermuseet (the Workers' Museum) this 'Café and Beer Hall' offers and impressive *smørrebrød* buffet. Be sure to take only two platters at a time but return as many times as you want. **$$**

Det Lille Apotek Store Kannikestræde 15, Copenhagen K; https://detlilleapotek.dk. Just a short walk from the Round Tower, 'The Little Pharmacy' is Copenhagen's oldest restaurant – Hans Christian Andersen is said to have dined here. It serves delicious Danish food – try the deluxe lunch-plate selection, or the juicy roast pork with crackling. **$$**

Geranium Per Henrik Lings Allé 4, Copenhagen Ø; www.geranium.dk. This three Michelin-starred restaurant was ranked second best in the world by *Restaurant* magazine in 2021 (trailing *Noma*), then followed that up the next year by taking the number one slot. The food is organic, seasonal and beautifully presented, though in a rather odd location: on the 8th floor of the national football stadium, Parken, affording it wonderful city views. Reservations required. **$$$$**

Restaurant Godt Gothersgade 38, Copenhagen K; www.restaurant-godt.dk. 'Godt' means good, an understatement for this small and friendly, family-run restaurant in the centre of town. Cuisine is mostly French, with a 3–5 course daily menu and a good selection of wines. **$$$$**

Orangeriet Kronprinsessegade 13, Copenhagen K; www.restaurant-orangeriet.dk. The setting makes this restaurant – its terrace and bank of windows look out over the beautiful Kongens Have gardens. It's pricey, but on a summer's day, it's a winner for a traditional *smørrebrød* lunch. **$$$**

Nyhavn and Beyond

Lumskebugten Esplanaden 21, Copenhagen K; www.lumskebugten.dk. A small and exclusive restaurant by Churchill Park near the Little Mermaid statue, with fine food and fine wine. Vegetarians can delight in their own three-course menu. Reservations are essential. **$$$**

Nyhavns Færgekro Nyhavns Færgekro, Nyhavn 5, Copenhagen K; www.nyhavnsfaergekro.dk. An unpretentious restaurant serving particularly good traditional food. It's renowned for its all-you-can-eat herring buffet, with the fish prepared in 10 different ways, accompanied by no less than 20 kinds of *snaps*. The picturesque location alongside Nyhavn is wonderful; you can choose to sit inside or out on the terrace depending on the weather. **$$**

Pastis Gothersgade 52, Copenhagen K; https://bistro-pastis.dk. Locals rate this brasserie, near Kongens Nytorv, for its cosy ambiance and concise menu of fiercely French favourites – snails, *lapin provençal*, *profiteroles*. The set menu is good value for this standard of cooking and includes a great selection of desserts. **$$**

Zeleste Store Strandstræde 6, Copenhagen K; https://zeleste.dk. This delightful little restaurant is tucked away just off Nyhavn – look for the great big kitsch shrimp outside. In summer eat out in the courtyard; in winter, the small traditional rooms are appealingly cosy. If you've come with an appetite, consider the seafood platter, a mountain of shrimp, oysters and Norwegian lobster. **$$**

Christianshavn and Holmen

Alchemist Refshalevej 173C, Copenhagen K; https://alchemist.dk. It's well worth the trip to Refshalevej for restaurant, claimant of two Michelin stars, its innovative founding chef Rasmus Munk ever determined to climb to new culinary heights. A meal here is not for the faint of heart; expect it to last from four to six hours, divided into dramatic acts comprised of some 50 edible 'impressions' in total. **$$$$**

La Banchina Refshalevaj 141, Copenhagen K; www.labanchina.dk. Eat, drink, swim and sweat at this charmingly casual restaurant and wine bar on the water, complete with on-site sauna. On sunny summer days, the deck is packed with locals soaking up the sun. **$$**

Kadeau Wildersgade 10BC, Copenhagen K; www.kadeau.dk. Its cuisine and décor inspired by the beloved Baltic isle of Bornholm (home to the original branch), Kadeau has two Michelin stars for good reason. Its inventive dishes include locally sourced octopus, beetroot and pork belly, as well as indigenous grains and berries. **$$$$**

Spiseloppen Badsmandsstræde 43, Christiania, Copenhagen K; https://spiseloppen.dk. The high quality of the cuisine at this rustic Christiania collective may come as a surprise after climbing its ramshackle staircase. There's a daily changing menu influenced by styles and flavours from all over the world. **$$**

Nørrebro

Ali Bageri Heimdalsgade 39, Copenhagen N; https:// alibageri.dk. A Copenhagen institution (with a second branch near Nørrebro Station), this is the go-to place for a traditional Lebanese breakfast platter. Chaotic at first glance, the restaurant is a well-oiled machine pumping out delicious manaish, fatteh and some of the tastiest hummus outside of the Levant. Save room for a piece of bakhlava and perhaps plan to skip lunch. **$**

Mirabelle Guldbergsgade 29, Copenhagen N; www.mirabelle-spiseria.dk. Blending Scandinavian and Sicilian flavours in gorgeous, airy surrounds, this long-time bakery opened its doors as a restaurant and wine-bar in 2023. It's best known for its breakfast and brunch, though it also serves a la carte lunches and dinners. Choices include beef tartar, arancini and pistachio pesto linguine. **$$**

Kiin Kiin Guldbergsgade 21, Copenhagen N; https://kiin.dk. 'Eat Eat' in Thai, this restaurant on trendy Sankt Hans Square in Nørrebro has earned rave reviews in the Danish media, having been the very first Thai restaurant in the world to earn a Michelin star. The set tasting menu is made up of creative dishes exploding with flavour. **$$$$**

Radio Julius Thomsens Gade 12, Copenhagen V; https://restaurantradio.dk. On the border of Frederiksberg and Nørrebro, near the Forum Metro station, Radio has won endless plaudits from the Danish media for its excellent, seasonal cuisine. While it's the brainchild of Claus Meyer, co-founder of the world-famous restaurant *Noma* (see box, page 105), prices are surprisingly down-to-earth, kept that way by packing in the tables and turning over several sittings every night. **$$**

Silberbauers Bistro Jægersborggade 40, Copenhagen V; www.silberbauers.dk. Just months after opening in 2021, this refreshingly laid-back bistro and wine bar earned Michelin praise (Bib Gourmand). Named for the owner and head chef, it serves excellent-value French cuisine from an ever-changing blackboard menu where seafood most often stars. **$$**

Travel essentials

Practical information

Accessible Travel

The Danes are generally very thoughtful about the needs of travellers with disabilities. God Adgang (www.godadgang.dk) is an Accessibility Label Scheme that keeps a searchable database of hotels, restaurants, shops, performance venues and tourist attractions that are accessible to people with disabilities.

Trains are equipped with lifts and ramps, and have disabled toilets. All Metro stations have lifts and most buses have collapsible ramps for the middle doors and a call button.

Accommodation

Most of Copenhagen's hotels are clustered near the city's main sights – Rådhuspladsen, Tivoli Gardens, the University Quarter and the lively shopping area along Strøget. It is always advisable to reserve well ahead of your stay. The city is at its busiest in the summer months (June–August), but conferences ensure that hotels are kept busy throughout the year.

Beyond its hotels, Copenhagen has little in the way of purpose-built holiday apartments. Local laws have ensured that the city's hundreds of Airbnb listings (airbnb.com) are technically limited to people's lived-in homes, giving many a distinctive charm (and a sense of *hygge*) that you won't easily find at a hotel. Alternatively, find rooms in private homes through Dansk Bed & Breakfast (www.bedandbreakfast.dk); but note that, in spite of the name, breakfast is rarely included! For longer stays, consider an apartment listed by the Hay 4 You agency (Knabrostræde 15, ground floor; www.hay4you.com).

Travellers on a budget can choose from an impressive number of excellent-value hostels scattered in the centre, with Steel House (Herholdtsgade 6; www.steelhousecopenhagen.com) and Generator (Adelgade 5-7; www.staygenerator.com) among the best of these.

How much is a room for one person/two people? **Hvad koster et enkeltværelse/dobbeltværelse?**
Is breakfast included? **Er der morgenmad?**

Airport

Copenhagen Airport, Kastrup (CPH; www.cph.dk), around 10km (6 miles) southeast of the city centre, is northern Europe's largest hub.

There are trains every 10 minutes to Hovedbanegård, Copenhagen's Central Station; and the Metro runs roughly every 4–6 minutes (15–20 minutes at night) into the city centre. Both leave from Terminal 3 (where all passengers go for baggage reclaim and customs), take about 14 minutes and cost 38kr. Buses (no. 5A) run less frequently and take about 30–35 minutes.

Taxis take 20–30 minutes; expect to pay 250–300kr, depending on the time of day.

Apps

The Copenhagen App (www.visitorservice.kk.dk). Enjoy personalized lists of attractions, restaurants and events across the city, courtesy of the municipality.

Donkey Republic (www.donkey.bike). App for Copenhagen's most widespread bike rental scheme.

Dot (www.publictransport.dk). Bus, train and metro app offering both single tickets and City Passes (available for 24, 48, 72, 96 or 120 hours).

Rejsekort (rejsekort.dk). Released in 2024, this is the local favourite app for public transport: simply swipe to check in and check out on buses, metro trains and harbour buses.

Bicycle Rental

Donkey Republic (donkey.bike) has a fleet of orange bikes which can be hired on a pay-as-you-go or monthly basis (first half hour is free). Many hotels offer guests free bicycles. Bikes can be put on S-tog trains except during rush hours. Look for carriages with a cycle symbol. Always be sure to signal and keep right on the bike paths.

Budgeting for Your Trip

Drinks. Beer 30–50kr; glass of wine from 60kr; soft drinks 30kr.

Hotels (double room with bath, including tax and service, high-season rates): 5-star from 2500kr, 4-star 1600kr, 3-star 1100kr, 2-star 900kr, 1-star 700kr. Dorm beds start around 275kr.
Meals: Light lunch 50–80kr, three course dinner with wine in a good establishment 400kr plus, coffee 25–40kr. Many restaurants offer a good-value *dagens ret* (daily special).
Museums: Many museums (including the National Museum) are free, or have one day a week where admission is free. Otherwise, entrance generally ranges from 100–150kr.
Public transport: 20kr for a single ticket on public transport.

Car Hire (see also Driving)

Having a car in Copenhagen is a hindrance rather than a help. The public-transport system is superb, and car rental, fuel and parking costs are quite high.

If you decide to hire a car once you are in Copenhagen, contact Avis (www.avis.dk); Europcar (www.europcar.dk); Hertz (www.hertzdk.dk); or Budget (www.budget.dk). Alternatively, Green Mobilty (www.greenmobility.com) offers rental by the hour, with cars parked all over the city and unlocked upon pickup via an app. You will need a valid national (or international) driving licence and must be at least 19 years of age (25 for some companies). Most agencies require payment by credit card.

Climate

Denmark's relatively temperate climate is due to its situation and the sea currents, but frequent switches in the wind also bring changeable weather. Spring may come late, but summer is often sunny and autumn mild. You can check the weather forecast at www.dmi.dk.

Average monthly temperatures in Copenhagen are:

	J	F	M	A	M	J	J	A	S	O	N	D
ºC	0	0	2	7	12	16	18	17	14	9	5	3
ºF	32	32	36	45	54	61	64	63	57	48	41	37

Crime and Safety (See also Emergencies and Police)

Copenhagen remains one of the safest capital cities in Europe. Pickpocketing rises during the summer months: take normal precautions, particularly in crowded areas.

Driving

If you take your car into Denmark from the UK then you will need a valid driver's licence, car registration papers, a Green Card, a red warning triangle in case of breakdown and a national identity sticker for your car. British car-owners should note that left-dipping headlights are illegal. Headlights are compulsory at all hours. Drive on the right, pass on the left.

Drinking and driving. The law is stringent: if you are discovered to have a blood-alcohol content of more than 0.05 percent while driving, you face severe penalties.

Electricity

The supply for electrical appliances in Denmark is 220-volt, 50 Hz AC, and requires standard two-pin, round continental plugs. Visitors should bring their own adaptors.

Embassies and Consulates

The embassies, with consulate sections, are generally open Mon–Fri 8am–4pm, but there is usually a 24-hour telephone service. New Zealand does not have an embassy in Denmark.

Australia: embassy: Dampfærgevej 26, 2nd floor, DK-2100 Copenhagen Ø; tel: 70 26 36 76; www.denmark.embassy.gov.au.

Canada: embassy: Kristen Bernikowsgade 1, DK-1105 Copenhagen K; tel: 33 48 32 00; international.gc.ca.

Republic of Ireland: embassy: Østbanegade 21, DK-2100 Copenhagen Ø; tel: 35 47 32 00; www.ireland.ie/en/denmark/copenhagen.

South Africa: embassy: Strandøre 15, DK-2100 Copenhagen Ø; tel: 39 18 01 85; www.dirco.gov.za/copenhagen.

UK: embassy: Kastelsvej 36–40, DK-2100 Copenhagen Ø; www.gov.uk/

world/organisations/british-embassy-copenhagen.
USA: embassy and consulate: Dag Hammarskjölds Allé 24, DK-2100 Copenhagen Ø; tel: 33 41 71 00; https://dk.usembassy.gov.

Emergencies (See also Police and Health and Medical Care)

The all-purpose emergency number is 112. Ask for police, fire or ambulance. Speak distinctly (English will be understood) and state your number and location.

There is a 24-hour, 365-day helpline staffed by nurses who can advise on medical questions, and tell you which emergency clinic has the shortest waiting time – tel: 1813.
Dental emergency. Tandlægevagten, Oslo Plads 14, tel: 1813 or 70 25 00 41, is a walk-in centre for out-of-hours dental emergencies, open Mon–Fri 8–9.30pm, Sat–Sun and public holidays 10am–noon and 8–9.30pm.

Can I use your phone? **Må jeg låne din telefon?**
I have lost my bag/wallet. **Jeg har mistet min taske/pung.**

Getting There

Air travel. The following airlines are among those operating regular services to Copenhagen **from the UK** (the phone numbers given are for calling from the UK): SAS (Scandinavian Airlines System; www.flysas.com), Norwegian Air (www.norwegian.com), British Airways (www.britishairways.com), easyJet (www.easyjet.com) and Ryanair (www.ryanair.com).
From the USA and Canada: SAS (Scandinavian Airlines System; www.flysas.com) operates daily flights to Copenhagen from Chicago, Newark, Washington and San Francisco. Air Canada (www.aircanada.com) has a regular service from Toronto.
From Australia and New Zealand: Flights to Copenhagen necessitate two, sometimes three, changes, usually in the Far East and then Europe.
Rail travel. To reach Copenhagen from London, first take the Eurostar from St Pancras International to Brussels (www.eurostar.com), then via Cologne

and Hamburg to Copenhagen. The journey from Brussels can be booked through Deutsche Bahn (https://int.bahn.de). Book the entire trip via Trainline (www.thetrainline.com).

Guides and Tours

The Association of Authorised Guides offers individual and group tours (Nørregade 41; www.guides.dk; Mon, Tues, Thur 10am–noon).

Canal and harbour tours. Canal Tours Copenhagen (www.stromma.dk) and Netto Boats (www.havnerundfart.dk) run 60-minute guided canal tours mid-January to mid-December, with around two to five departures per hour. Boats run from 10am to 7pm in July and Aug, shorter hours during the rest of the year. Canal Tours Copenhagen boats depart from Nyhavn and Gammel Strand; Netto tours depart from Nyhavn and Holmens Church. Strömma also runs the 'hop-on-hop-off' boat, with a free audioguide.

City tours. City Sightseeing (www.stromma.dk) 'hop-on-hop-off' bus tours are good-value (City Hall Square) five minutes past the hour from 9am to 2pm. The company also runs City & Harbour Tours, combined bus-and-boat tours. Tickets are valid from 1 to 48 hours. Politically Incorrect Tours (www.politicallyincorrectfreetours.com) offer "free" (tip-based), English-language guided walks through various parts of the city, inflected with a heavy dose of local humour, generally lasting 90 minutes.

Cycling and running. Several companies offer guided bike tours, including a three-hour whiz round the city with Bike-Mike (www.bikecopenhagenwithmike.dk). For energetic types there are also jogging tours (try https://gorunningtours.com).

Health and Medical Care

EU citizens with a European Health Insurance Card (EHIC) are entitled to necessary treatment during their stay in Denmark. The same applies for UK citizens with a UK-issued Global Health Insurance Card (GHIC). In all cases, full travel insurance is still advised, and be sure to hold on to receipts.

A Danish pharmacy *(apotek)* is strictly a dispensary. Opening hours are generally Mon–Fri 9am–5.30pm, Sat until 1pm. An all-night service operates at Steno Apotek, Vesterbrogade 6C, tel: 33 14 82 66, near the main train station.

I need a doctor/dentist. **Jeg har brug for en læge/tandlæge.**

Language

English is widely spoken and understood. Danish is almost impossible to pronounce simply by reading the words, as many syllables are swallowed rather than spoken. Thus the island of Amager becomes Am-air, with the 'g' disappearing, but in a distinctively Danish way difficult for the visitor to imitate. The letter 'd' becomes something like a 'th', but with the tongue placed behind the lower teeth, not the upper. The letter 'y' is like the 'ee' in 'see', but spoken with rounded lips as if making an 'o'. The letter 'ø' is like the 'u' in the English 'nurse' but spoken with the lips far forward. That said, the same vowel isn't always pronounced the same way. There are only nine written vowels but 22 different vowel sounds.

There are 29 letters in the Danish alphabet including 'æ' (as in egg), 'ø', and 'å' (as in port). They appear after the usual 26 (a point to note when looking up names in phone books and lists).

Days

Monday **mandag**
Tuesday **tirsdag**
Wednesday **onsdag**
Thursday **torsdag**
Friday **fredag**
Saturday **lørdag**
Sunday **søndag**

Months

January **januar**
February **februar**
March **marts**
April **april**
May **maj**
June **juni**
July **juli**
August **august**
September **september**
October **oktober**
November **november**
December **december**

Numbers

0 **nul**
1 **en**
2 **to**
3 **tre**
4 **fire**
5 **fem**
6 **seks**
7 **syv**
8 **otte**
9 **ni**
10 **ti**
11 **elleve**
12 **tolv**
13 **tretten**
14 **fjorten**

15 **femten**
16 **seksten**
17 **sytten**
18 **atten**
19 **nitten**
20 **tyve**
30 **tredive**
40 **fyrre**
50 **halvtreds**
60 **tres**
70 **halvfjerds**
80 **firs**
90 **halvfems**
100 **hundrede**
1000 **tusind**

LGBTQ+ Travel

Denmark was the world's first country to recognise same-sex partnerships and Centralhjørnet (www.centralhjornet.dk), in Copenhagen, is the world's oldest existing gay bar. The city has a thriving LGBTQ+ scene, with bars, clubs and hotels openly welcoming the gay community. The annual Copenhagen Pride week takes place in August, culminating in a Saturday parade.

Lost Property

The general lost-property office *(hittegodskontor)* is at the police station at Politigården (tel: 38 74 88 22; Mon–Fri 9am–2pm). For property lost on trains, contact the S-train information office (tel: 70 10 14 15; daily 9am–11am).

Money

Currency. The unit of Danish currency is the kroner, abbreviated to kr, or, abroad, DKK (to distinguish it from the Norwegian and Swedish kroner). It is divided into 100 øre. Coins: 50 øre; 1, 2, 5, 10 and 20 kroner. Banknotes: 50, 100, 200 and 500 kroner. With certain exceptions, businesses are required by law to accept cash though it is rarely used in practice; indeed, when presented with tangible currency, younger Danes may react with confusion.

Credit cards. Credit cards are universally accepted, increasingly via contactless payment. ATMs are plentiful in the centre; use the machines outside official bank branches, avoiding those inside kiosks (where withdrawal fees are generally high).

Tax. Danish VAT is called MOMS and is set at 25 percent. It's always included in the bill. Foreign visitors can claim a tax refund if they spend over 300kr in a single shop displaying the Global Tax-Free Shopping sign. Ask the cashier for a tax-free form, then take it to Planet Payment (www.planetpayment.com) or Global Blue (www.globalblue.com), who have desks in the airport and the large department stores, for a 20 percent refund. Alternatively, you can post your tax-free form.

Opening Times

Banks. Open Mon–Fri 10am–6pm, Thu until 5.30pm. In the provinces, hours fluctuate from town to town.

Museums. Often closed on Monday and generally open for shorter hours during the winter. Most museums open 10am–5pm.

Shops. Hours vary from business to business, but general opening times are Mon–Thu 10am–6pm, Fri 9am–8pm, Sat 9am–5pm; supermarkets, some boutiques and corner shops are also open on Sun. Many restaurants close on Monday and Sundays.

Police (See also Emergencies)

State and city police all form part of the national force and are dressed in dark-blue uniforms. Most policemen patrol in dark-blue-and-white or white cars with the word *politi* in large letters. Police are courteous and speak English.

The all-purpose emergency number is 112. For non-emergencies, you can also phone 114 to be connected to the nearest local police station. Main Copenhagen police station: Politigården, Polititorvet 1, tel: 33 14 14 48.

Where's the nearest police station? **Hvor er den nærmeste politi-station?**

Post Offices

Post offices are set within supermarkets (look for the light blue counters and the Postnord logo, featuring a bugle capped with a crown).

Public Holidays

Though Denmark's banks, offices and major shops close on public holidays, museums, cafés and tourist attractions will mostly be open. Although Christmas Eve and New Year's Eve are not official holidays, most shops, businesses and attractions close on those days too.

1 January Nytårsdag New Year's Day
5 June (half-day) Grundslovsdag Constitution Day
25/26 December Christmas
Moveable dates:
Skærtorsdag Maundy Thursday
Langfredag Good Friday
Anden påskedag Easter Monday
Kristi himmelfartsdag Ascension Day
Anden pinsedag Whit Monday

Telephones

The country code for Denmark is 45. Local Danish numbers have eight digits, and there are no area codes.

To call Denmark from the UK: dial 00 + 45 + the personal telephone number.

To make international calls from Denmark: dial 00 + the country code

+ the area code (omitting the first 0 for UK numbers) + the personal telephone number.

Mobile phones. Copenhagen and Zealand are amply covered by both 4G and 5G networks. Mobile phone use in EU countries is now included in most plans for no extra cost but it's advisable to check with your local provider for information on roaming costs before visiting. Alternatively, consider purchasing a prepaid local SIM card at the airport or an eSIM in advance to save time on arrival.

Time Zones

Denmark operates on Central European Time (GMT + 1). In summer, the clock is put one hour ahead (GMT + 2). The time differences are:

New York	London	**Copenhagen**	Jo'burg	Sydney
7am	noon	**1pm**	1pm	9pm

Tipping

Tipping is not obligatory in Denmark, as most hotel and restaurant staff are paid proper salaries.

Toilets

Facilities are usually indicated by a pictograph; alternatively they are marked WC, *Toiletter, Damer/Herrer* (Ladies/Gentlemen), or just D/H. There is no charge unless you see it clearly marked otherwise.

Tourist Information

The Copenhagen Visitor Centre, 4a Vesterbrogade, across from Central Station and just outside Tivoli (Oct–Feb Mon–Sat 9am–4pm, Sun 9am–2pm, Mar–Apr daily 9am–4pm, May–June and Sept Mon–Sat 9am–6pm, Sun 9am–4pm, July–Aug Mon–Fri 9am–8pm, Sat–Sun 9am–6pm, tel: 70 22 24 42; www.visitcopenhagen.com), offers a comprehensive array of tourist information, and assistance with booking sightseeing tours and accommodation.

The Copenhagen Visitor Centre is also one of the many places where you can purchase the Copenhagen Card (www.copenhagencard.com), potentially offering good value, though this is dependent on which sights you'll see and how much public transport you'll use. The all-inclusive variety is the Discover Card, offering admission to 80+ attractions in addition to covering public transport (including to the airport) and up to two children for free. The 24/48/72/96/120-hour cards cost 499/739/919/1069/1199kr (children 10–15 years 279/399/489/579/649kr), and two children under 10 years may accompany each adult free of charge.

UK: VisitDenmark, e-mail: london@visitdenmark.com; www.visitdenmark.com.

Transport

An excellent integrated public-transport system covers not only Copenhagen but also its extensive metropolitan area. The area is divided into zones, with fares charged according to how many zones you pass through. The system makes travel simple: the same tickets are used on buses, S-trains, the harbour bus and the Metro. A basic ticket permits travel within two zones for one hour and costs 24kr (12kr for children aged 0–15; a paying adult can bring two children under 12 for free). Single tickets and city passes (available for 24, 48, 72, 96 or 120 hours) are available in the DOT mobile app (publictransport.dk). Alternatively, download the Rejsekort app and simply swipe to check in and out.

Buses. Operated by Movia (www.moviatrafik.dk), buses run daily between 6am and 12.30am. There are additional night buses from Rådhuspladsen to the suburbs. Buses are yellow and you get on at the front and off at the back. On C-buses (the 5C, for instance), however, passengers enter at the back.

Harbour Bus. The blue-and-yellow boats (www.moviatrafik.dk) run six times an hour (6am–6pm) through the harbour, between the Royal Library on Christians Brygge and the Little Mermaid, with stops at Nyhavn and Holmen North.

Metro. Automated Metro trains (http://intl.m.dk) run on four lines – M1,

M2 (linking the airport), M3 and M4 (linking Sydhavn) – every 4–6 minutes in the daytime, and every 15–20 minutes through the night.

S-Train. Operated by DSB S-Tog (www.dsb.dk), the red S-tog local trains connect Copenhagen with other towns on Sjælland.

Taxis. Taxis are recognisable by a *Taxi* or *Taxa* sign, and vacant cabs display the word *fri* (free). All drivers use a meter. Tipping is not necessary, but round the sum up if you are impressed by the service. Fares are quite high and considerably higher at night. Most drivers accept credit cards. Neither Uber nor lyft is available in Denmark. Viggo (www.viggo.dk) is the only taxi app. Phone numbers of taxi companies include 48 48 48 48 and 35 35 35 35.

Trains. A comprehensive and generally punctual network, which covers the entire country, operates from Copenhagen Central Station.

How much is a ticket to...? **Hvad koster en billet til...?**
One ticket to..., please. **En billet til..., tak.**
Where does this train/bus go? **Hvor kører dette tog/denne bus hen?**

Visas and Entry Requirements

Visitors from Britain and countries outside the EU need a valid passport to enter Denmark; citizens from EU countries (excluding Britain) need only an identity card. Visitors from the UK, USA, EU, Australia and New Zealand are generally entitled to stay in Denmark for up to 90 days without a visa. South African citizens need a visa. See the Danish Embassy in South Africa website for further information: www.sydafrika.um.dk.

Index

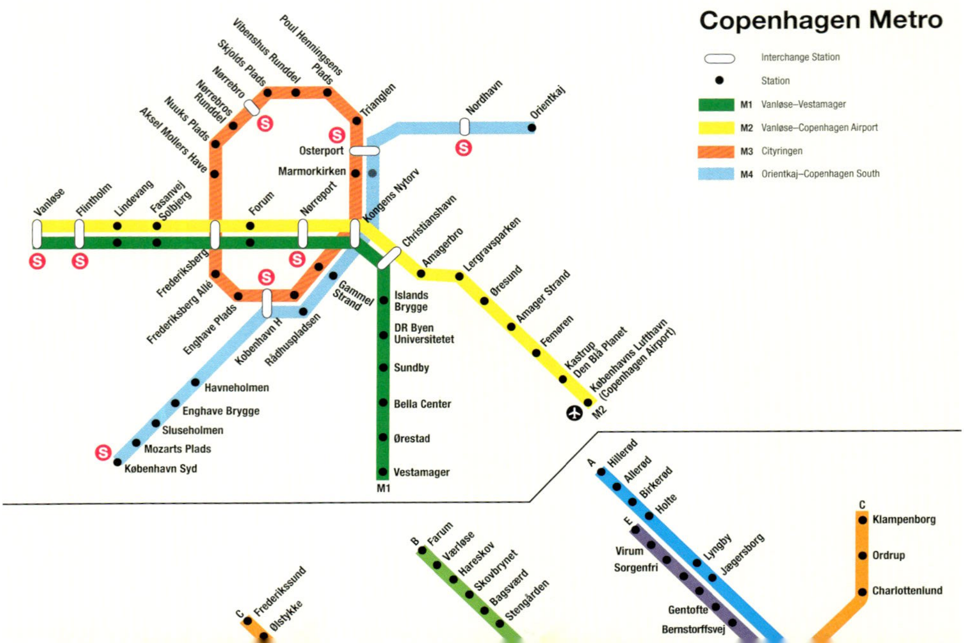

Copenhagen Metro
Interchange Station
Station
M1 Vanløse–Vestamager
M2 Vanløse–Copenhagen Airport
M3 Cityringen
M4 Orientkaj–Copenhagen South
Vanløse
Flintholm
Lindevang
Fasanvej Solbjerg
Forum
Nørreport
Kongens Nytorv
Christianshavn
Amagerbro
Lergravsparken
Øresund
Amager Strand
Femøren
Kastrup
Den Blå Planet
Københavns Lufthavn (Copenhagen Airport)
M2
Islands Brygge
DR Byen Universitetet
Sundby
Bella Center
Ørestad
Vestamager
M1
Frederiksberg
Frederiksberg Allé
Enghave Plads
København H
Rådhuspladsen
Gammel Strand
Marmorkirken
Osterport
Trianglen
Poul Henningsens Plads
Vibenshus Runddel
Skjolds Plads
Nørrebro
Nørrebros Runddel
Nuuks Plads
Aksel Møllers Have
Nordhavn
Orientkaj
Havneholmen
Enghave Brygge
Sluseholmen
Mozarts Plads
København Syd
A
Hillerød
Allerød
Birkerød
Holte
Lyngby
Jægersborg
E
Virum
Sorgenfri
Gentofte
Bernstorffsvej
C
Klampenborg
Ordrup
Charlottenlund
B
Farum
Værløse
Hareskov
Skovbrynet
Bagsværd
Stengården
C
Frederikssund
Ølstykke

Copenhagen S-tog (S-train)
Interchange Station
A Køge – Hillerød
B Høje Taastrup – Farum
Bx Høje Taastrup – Buddinge
C Frederikssund – Klampenborg
E Køge – Holte
F Ny Ellebjerj – Hellerup
H Ballerup– Østerport
Hellerup
Svanemøllen
Nordhavn
Østerport
Nørreport
Vesterport
København H
Dybbølsbro
Carlsberg
Valby
Sydhavn
Sjælør
Ny Ellebjerg
Åmarken
Friheden
Avedøre
Brøndby Strand
Vallensbæk
Ishøj
Hundige
Greve
Karlslunde
Solrød Strand
Jersie
Køge Nord
Ølby
Køge
Vigerslev Allé
Danshøj
Hvidovre
Rødovre
Glostrup
Albertslund
Taastrup
Høje Taastrup
Bx
B
KB Hallen
Ålholm
Langgade
Peter Bangs Vej
Flintholm
Vanløse
Jyllingevej
Islev
Husum
Herlev
Skovlunde
Malmparken
Ballerup
Måløv
Veksø
Stenløse
Egedal
H
Grøndal
Fuglebakken
Nørrebro
Bispebjerg
Ryparken
F
Emdrup
Dyssegård
Vangede
Kildebakke
Buddinge
Bx

THE **MINI** ROUGH GUIDE TO **COPENHAGEN**

First Edition 2025

Editor: Beth Williams
Author: Anthon Jacksn
Picture Editor: Piotr Kala
Picture Manager: Tom Smyth
Cartography Update: Katie Bennett
Layout: Grzegorz Madejak
Production Operations Manager: Katie Bennett
Publishing Technology Manager: Rebeka Davies
Head of Publishing: Sarah Clark
Photography Credits: Anders Kjærbye/Copenhagen Media Center 100; Astrid Maria Rasmussen/Copenhagen Media Center 104; Büro Jantzen/Copenhagen Media Center 108; Cees van Roeden/Copenhagen Media Center 47; Daniel Rasmussen/Copenhagen Media Center 28, 30; David Hall/Apa Publications 14CL; Dianne Pavletich/Copenhagen Media Center 1; Glyptoteket/Copenhagen Media Center 53; iStock 7, 13CB, 32, 64, 68, 70, 102; Mark Tanggaard/Visit Copenhagen 90; Morten Jerichau/Copenhagen Media Center 55, 73; Public domain 25, 26; Rudy Hemmingsen/Apa Publications 92; Shutterstock 4, 8, 11, 12CL, 12TL, 12BL, 12CR, 12BR, 13T, 13CT, 13CB, 14T, 14BR, 16T, 16CL, 16BR, 16BL, 18T, 18CL, 18BR, 18BL, 21, 23, 34, 36, 38, 41, 43, 45, 49, 51, 56, 59, 61, 63, 66, 67, 72, 75, 76, 79, 80, 83, 84, 87, 89, 96, 97, 99, 109, 113; Thomas Høyrup Christensen/Copenhagen Media Center 13B; Thomas Ibsen/Copenhagen Media Center 106; Ty Stange/Copenhagen Media Center 14BL, 95; Wonderful Copenhagen 110, 114
Cover Credits: Nyhavn **iStock**

About the author

Anthon Jackson is an American, Denmark-based writer and photographer. He has contributed to more than 30 travel books for Rough Guides and other series. Find Anthon on Instagram @anthonjackson, on X @janthonjackson, and visit his website, www.anthonjackson.com.

Distribution
UK, Ireland and Europe: Apa Publications (UK) Ltd; sales@roughguides.com
United States and Canada: Ingram Publisher Services; ips@ingramcontent.com
Australia and New Zealand: Booktopia; retailer@booktopia.com.au
Worldwide: Apa Publications (UK) Ltd; sales@roughguides.com

Special Sales, Content Licensing and CoPublishing
Rough Guides can be purchased in bulk quantities at discounted prices. We can create special editions, personalised jackets and corporate imprints tailored to your needs. sales@roughguides.com; http://roughguides.com

Printed in Czech Republic

This book was produced using **Typefi** automated publishing software.

Contact us

Every effort has been made to provide accurate information in this publication, but changes are inevitable. The publisher cannot be held responsible for any resulting loss, inconvenience or injury sustained by any traveller as a result of information or advice contained in the guide. We would appreciate it if readers would call our attention to any errors or outdated information, or if you feel we've left something out. Please send your comments with the subject line "Rough Guide Mini Copenhagen Update" to mail@uk.roughguides.com.